"Reading *Writing From the Inside Out* is like bathing in a sea of words that connect with your soul and make you understand the true meaning behind what poetry is. This book is a stunning peek into the author's mind and heart as he shares and explores the life experiences he's had that contribute to his unique gift. Stephen takes you on a journey of what it is to write, what goes into the practice, the parallels between writing and yoga, the meditative approach, the idea of action, outlining your book, moving through and embracing the ego, and all along the way discovering your truth in the process. Absorbing the lessons in this book will add a dimension to your creative practice and make you a much stronger writer in the process."

> — Jen Grisanti, author: *Story Line* and *Change Your Story, Change Your Life*

"I urge others to write from the heart to find their true artistic voice. Here is a book that profoundly helps one explore that mysterious personal journey. A navigation guide to our inner creative magic."

> — Pen Densham, author: *Riding the Alligator*; screenwriter: *Robin Hood: Prince of Thieves*

"If you wish to learn the 'attentiveness' that Thoreau and Emerson felt was the essential quality of the writer, read Stephen Webber's break-through book, *Writing From the Inside Out*. Webber, a bold thinker and a searching, unconventional teacher of creative writing, gives you unique opportunities to significantly alter your processes of composing and revising every aspect of your work."

> — Kevin McIlvoy, author: *The Complete History of New Mexico & Other Stories*

"Somewhere inside this quietly-stocked storehouse of reflection and anecdotes, of sound advice and exercises, I found myself involuntarily re-centered — my crossed wires came gently uncrossed — the act of writing (and reading, and breathing) took on a freshness I'd forgotten. Webber likens the art of making art to 'meditation in the midst of action.' That's a mighty fine description of this truly helpful book."
— Joseph Scapellato, writer and teacher

"In *Writing From the Inside Out*, Webber reminds us that any and all pursuits such as yoga and writing are all a reach for realizing The One, and that all worldly pursuits seek what is beyond ourselves."
— Catherine Ann Jones, author of *The Way of Story* and *Heal Your Self with Writing*

"There are many frothy writing books. *Writing From the Inside Out* certainly is not one of them. Stephen Lloyd Webber's writing is charged, energetic. His chapters are surprisingly titled, his exercises fresh and inviting. As a writer and yoga practitioner, he brings new meaning to 'the body and mind are one.' Yoga and writing both require sustained attention and in this book Webber has paid very close attention. The language is poetic — 'garden-fresh' as he says in talking about what happens in the moment of creation. 'A Life With Poetry at its Center' is a chapter that calls all of us writers back to what we may have forgotten, if we ever knew it: 'poetry is the ethical stewardship of ideas.' There are two kinds of structure, he writes: supportive and musical. Webber's book has both. It's tight without being skeletal, robust without being overblown, and well worth every writer's attention."
— Karen Speerstra, author: *Sophia: The Feminine Face of God* and *Color: The Language of Light*

# writing
*from* **THE INSIDE OUT**

*the practice of* **FREE-FORM WRITING**

**STEPHEN LLOYD WEBBER**

DIVINE
ARTS

Published by DIVINE ARTS

DivineArtsMedia.com

An imprint of Michael Wiese Productions

12400 Ventura Blvd. #1111

Studio City, CA 91604

(818) 379-8799, (818) 986-3408 (FAX)

Cover Design: Johnny Ink. www.johnnyink.com

Book Layout: William Morosi

Copyeditor: Annalisa Zox-Weaver

Printed by McNaughton & Gunn, Inc., Saline, Michigan

Manufactured in the United States of America

Library of Congress Cataloging-in-Publication Data

Webber, Stephen Lloyd, 1982- author.

  Writing From the Inside Out : The Practice of Free-Form Writing / Stephen Lloyd Webber.

    pages cm

  ISBN 978-1-61125-015-2

  1. Free verse--Authorship. 2. Poetry--Authorship. 3. Creative writing. 4. Poetry, Modern. 5. Poetics. I. Title.

  PN1059.F7W43 2013

  808.1--dc23

                             2012040691

Printed on Recycled Stock

# CONTENTS

# 1. BLIND FAITH

# TURNING A PHRASE

> I wouldn't like to separate our mindfulness into two categories, one of which is your forty-minute daily ritual, which is "practice," and the other not practice. Practice simply is one intensification of what is natural and around us all of the time. Practice is to life as poetry is to spoken language. So as poetry is the practice of language, "practice" is the practice of life. But from the enlightened standpoint, all of language is poetry, all of life is practice. At any time when the attention is there fully, then all of the Bodhisattva's acts are being done.
>
> — GARY SNYDER

Several years ago, when I was attending Oklahoma State University as a creative writing major, I became acquainted with the poet Ai, and not long after that, I became her driver. For a couple of months, whenever she was going out of town, she'd give me a call. This went on until I graduated and left town myself. So for me many stories of Oklahoma are, in some way, about getting out of town.

I remember one instance in which I drove Ai to a Lawton library so she could research her Native American ancestry. While she spent hours doing this, I sat mesmerized under fluorescent lights at a long wooden table reading Julio Cortazar's *Rayuela*, that great body of writing that allows the reader to impose his or her own sequence on the chapters.

A couple of weeks later, I gave Ai a ride to a poetry reading she was giving in Dayton, Ohio. It was a fourteen-hour drive from Stillwater, and because she had a lot of anxiety associated with travel, we didn't even get started until midnight. She kept putting it off. Finally, we got out of town. I drove in silence. It was a big white extended cab diesel truck she'd rented from the school (safer than a car, I suppose). She didn't want to hear the radio, music, anything. We spoke occasionally of poetry. She said of my writing that they weren't true poems, but that I could really "turn a phrase." It wasn't the most useful criticism I'd received, but the thought resonated with me, nonetheless.

Over the years, I continued to write and make my own discoveries. I earned my MFA in poetry at New Mexico State University, and a couple of years later, I set a New Year's resolution to write twenty books in a year. Through the experience, I learned a lot about writing, and about myself.

With regard to my goal, I turned a phrase. I came to think about the resolution as "putting together twenty book-length projects," as opposed to "writing twenty books." The different turn of phrase gave me more flexibility to compile works, because I wasn't limiting myself to writing one book at a time from start to finish. I was sometimes working on six books at once, and I felt the freedom to write them in any order. I gained familiarity with modes of organization, and eventually each project snapped more or less into place. One major component of making this shift was that I was practicing yoga — particularly, pranayama and meditation — regularly. Prior to yoga, I had been active and in good shape, though my time at the gym wasn't necessarily the sort of physical activity that merged seamlessly with my writing practice. My life took an even stronger shift toward the contemplative when I went through a medical issue with the retinas in both of my eyes and, for several weeks, faced the possibility that I would go blind. Things that had once appeared important lost their charge; things that had once been difficult, I realized no longer needed to be so. I recentered my life around what I loved and tried to let go of the things I could not control.

Experience is our best teacher. More important than any writing "trick" is a creative approach that is true to life, trusting in the sufficiency of the present moment to contain the right expression. This approach means not trying to fit new material into familiar categories and not over-anticipating the result. While I recovered from the surgery that saved my vision, I couldn't be sure how things were going to turn out. Working creatively, I can't know the result in advance. I love abiding in uncertainty when it leads to a flash of recognition or a new idea. But if I hope to be sustainably productive, I need to appreciate the state of being that precedes intellectual recognition.

This is yoga: even-mindedness without attachment to what comes from heartfelt effort. It benefits me to recognize that my artistic expression is an extension of something already sufficient — perhaps already complete. Even when I am clear and wholly intentional, factors unknown to me are at work. Thoughts affect language, and language affects the movement of mind and body. There is a rhythm to language that is akin to the rhythm of thinking and the rhythm of breath. The linguistic landscape sometimes affects us more powerfully than the physical environment — when reading the first edition of *Leaves of Grass*, I'm apt to forget where I am.

Good writing is good medicine. When circumstances lead a writer through uncertainty into greater understanding, the phrases turn — and they turn the reader, enlivening the reader's perspective. Sometimes, depending on what comes before and after, a phrase can reveal or enact a compelling image, up-end our expectations, and continue to resonate with us. There can be a truth in turning phrases that exceeds my wildest expectations.

It is a gift that language itself, as a structured thing, is rather loose. There is more than one way to express a thing. When someone tells you to *inhale* and, in response, you breathe in, the body feels a certain way. Compare this action to how the body responds to the suggestion that you *let nature breathe into you*. Outwardly, the action is the same — you're still inhaling — but inwardly, the focus is different. This practice is language yoga — lucidly stretching, the mind and body experience freedom. Rather than trying to *make the mind calm*, rather than willfully trying to *stop thinking*, do this: *Watch the mind think*. Then: *Embody the witness*.

As a writer, I seek moments when phrases turn and images emerge and resonate. The result can't be anticipated. It is free-form writing. Just as yoga is not a means to a preconceived end — it is a practice to deepen devotion and transcend the self — so, too, can writing be. I also refer to this free-form approach as prose poetry — a mode of writing that feels like poetry even when it doesn't look like a poem.

Creativity is a continual and ongoing process, happening both inside and outside of me, intellectually and physically; nature is expressed all the time through all forms. Prose poetry asks that I live aware of this continual dreaming, whether I am writing or not. At the end of life, I will realize: There could be no greater gift than to have this sense of self. I am here in this moment in which one phrase turns into another; life's end may turn out much the same — one thing becoming another. My past conditioning, favorable or unfavorable, serves me, and my life's work pulls me forward. I am drawn to the images and experiences enacted by words for a reason that becomes more resolved in each moment.

The more open I am to what can emerge from my efforts, the better my ability is to make distinctions. A universal image resonates through all things, leaving no part out. As a writer who is writing, I resonate with that image, departing for the claim of thought or phrase, returning to find the moment fresh and lucid. By honoring the nuances of creativity that could appear to be nonessential, I am authentic to the circumstances that led me here, and so I create well, and I live in line with nature.

> ◢ *I wheeled with the stars,*
> *my heart broke free on the open sky.*
>
> — PABLO NERUDA

# A LIFE WITH POETRY AT ITS CENTER

> ◢ *Poetry is a physical art without a physical presence, so that it often finds itself in cadence to the heartbeat, the thud of days, and in the childish grasp of the reality of rhymes.*
>
> — RUSSELL EDSON

Beyond what gets written, poetry exists in sense experience, in everyday attention. There is a functional approach to living, whereby I go about driven by the things I have to do — too many responsibilities, day-to-day labors — and then there is the approach to life where I face the music. Outward forms change. Inward forms change. Life is full when I am roused by the desire to create.

As a writer, I find that this desire to create means tending the creative fields and harvesting the phrases that are presented to me. Mostly, it means being truly and deeply satisfied that there is always *more than enough*. In the present moment, magic always happens; creating work that reaches into the flow of this magic is its own fulfillment. When creativity smiles on my efforts, the result is a whole that is much greater than the sum of its parts.

The challenge would appear to be how to sustain my efforts in the face of all the stuff life hands me. The issue is more fundamental — it is *why* rather than *how*. The path finds me at the convergence of my natural abilities, what serves the world, and what I adore. Often, the trick is not so much finding time but finding heartspace to be productive and creatively effective. Poetry can live in many forms, but it won't come to the forefront if my heart is not in it. I disappear when I am devoted to my craft, sweating with the labor of love.

The creative moment is always the present one. The air I breathe is my call to action. It gives me the material I need to do my job, which is to stretch mindfully through corridors of prolonged weirdness and uncertainty to give voice to image. By unkinking doubt to embrace greater negative capability, I find better modes of organization.

One of the great wonders of my life is that I prioritize backwards, with art saved for later, after the bills are paid, after my world seems secure. More wonderful than this process is witnessing the self truly dripping with artistic creation. Living wholeheartedly, I devote my time, energy, my body — such as it is — to rendering forms that echo the truth of the soul — all with no promised external reward and no reality-anchor, except the love of pursuit — and, at times, no stability whatsoever but the momentum of continual practice.

Poetry is essential to society even when it is not functional — which is usually the case. In society, poetry conveys our myths, lives in every gesture and symbol, enacts compelling stories, and interacts with forms of beauty that nudge the sublime. Poetry calls the soul to express the sound of the world beyond. Poetry is to imagination what meditation is to attention.

If ideas are understood to have a life of their own, art and poetry are the ethical stewardship of those ideas. This stewardship is magnetic. There's the sensation of being drenched in creative juices. Sometimes it feels like the quality of light in early spring-time: afternoon with a slight breeze. I am outside, looking at the trees swaying in the light, and everything feels and looks natural; everything wears all-natural fibers. The pergola is wood — it feels alive. The roof is bamboo thatch, and a vine grows up it. The buds of fruit have started; they've just begun to enter this world from the domain of infinite possibility, the other side of things in the here-and-now. I've just awoken from a surprisingly restful nap. Red wine was involved beforehand. Before that was a good bout of manual labor in the garden. I'm in love. What woke me from the nap was the footfall of a bird exploring the front deck, pecking for seeds dropped from the crust of whole-grain bread. The golden light of sunshine has entered everything — sunlight filters through the screen door. It lights up the unassuming brown of the bird's feathers, revealing blue and golden hues. I feel seen but entirely unjudged — the bird has its eye on me, but all of my qualities don't enter the picture. I am a created thing, and what I signify to the bird feels as valid as anything for which I could ever strive. A towel swings in the breeze, drying — it's older than I am; my mother dried me with it before I had been capable of such things. Sunlight shines through its fibers, lighting it up and coloring its shadows.

Sometimes it's all too much to keep up with; I'm in the flow and outside of it. My senses are flooded, on the verge of being overwhelmed — too good to be true, too much to handle, and yet they continue to waterfall: ideas, good ideas, and in more or less the right order. I'm in a rushing stream, moving nimbly, chaotically — and the nearer I get to the verge of complete disaster — crashing into a boulder, plunging into a whirlpool, catapulting onto dry land — the more maddening it is as I see how luck favors me, and the way I end up going turns out to be the right way. One split-second decision follows another, and another, and there's no turning back, only the thrill of getting lost on the path I've been presented. My fuel, frighteningly, is inexhaustible. The roar of waves and of my own full-tilt breath converge at the summit of what I hear.

Sometimes I have to fall asleep before the real unconscious work can happen. A mathematician's trick is to pose short-term memory at the apex of an unsolved problem, and then take a nap. While asleep, the brain does work for which the conscious mind usually doesn't have the resources. A simple departure into the imagination links two worlds. Beyond reverie is a realm where things appear very different and have nothing of the stability or persistence of physical objects in the here-and-now. Time moves across a different span; there are no natural rules and laws — not so much anyway. Math plays around in the land of unlimited resources. It is enlivening to bring it more into communion with the iceberg of this waking world, where commerce and routine speak loudly against the unconscious. I must be certain that a dollar bill is not folded into an origami swan when paying for parking. And, in this sphere, a finite number of dollar bills is available to me. How would things be different if that were not the observable truth? This is the stuff of dreams and of imagination, very unlike the life of presumed certainty.

What would life be like if I gave up everything and attended only to the few things that provide me with the most charge? If I minimized my faith in the redemptive aspects of the well-commerced life, the full-time job, the hope for retirement, and acted creatively on the page and amid it all? If I prioritized quality of life based on a rich attention span and a sense of communion with the naturally imaginative world?

I want no one to delay his or her work that is an expression of oneness. For me, the only right way to live is the way that has poetry at its center. The word "poetry" has its roots in the ancient Greek word *poiesis,* a verb that means "to make." Poetry is the path of authentic articulation; this life works to express the wisdom and sublime beauty of union between the self and wild nature.

The life that embraces uncertainty worships the unmanifest as it takes form. The poetry that is mine depends on what shapes my motivation. It is good to be ambitious — yet I do a bit of a disservice to the creative impulse by claiming my predispositions as though I consciously formed them. The craft of writing enters my life; I am grateful. It fits and challenges me. I invite it more intimately into my life than any other pursuit and adopt it as a practice. Trying it out becomes commitment, and then a dance, as it takes me for a ride as much as the other way around. The relationship itself governs what happens. Acting spontaneously — whether tightly or loosely — is the poetry of the moment.

Poetry holds a unique position among the arts. It emerges as a material or energetic presence, but is without physical form. When shaping a poem, I'm not shaping anything but words on a page and phrases in the rhythm of thought. Take sculpture as an example: There's a stone, and I carve away at the stone; or, there's a bit of wire, and I bend the wire. Take music as an example.

There's an instrument, and I relate to the instrument in a way that produces vibrations. With poetry, there's no paint, but there is an image. No two objects are striking each other, yet there is resonance. The resonance comes from the way we engage with language; it's from the words, their texture and connotation, and from the friction of experience.

What I celebrate when I love poetry is not entirely the written or spoken word. Rather, I celebrate language through the words; I celebrate the quality of attention that makes a poem. I celebrate the imagination as organized by a body. I celebrate my relationship to language, and how words reunite me with imagination and wonder.

I take language to be my instrument, and language shapes me as much as I interact with it. The words I use come to me. They are an offering from the imagination. The real art of poetry is in what occurs prior to locating the foothold offered by having acquired language. In that place of constantly varying music, we behold the incarnation of the original image. In the moment, the coiled rope is also the serpent, whether it is later to be beheld as serpent or rope. All is recognized to be numinous and alive. Prior to hearing language's footfall, I am in the domain of spirits, whether I believe I am or not.

## STEWARDS OF ENERGY

At its essence, practicing poetry or free-form writing means being curious, giving some shape to enlivening patterns of thought without building a framework of undue familiarity. Instead, I grow a winding lattice of curiosity. Something drives me to a certain kind of work. And so I do it. Periodically, I check in to see what is happening based on my efforts.

In the way of inspiration, the most I can ever do is create the place for it to happen. I can't light the spark, but I can create the dry and fragrant kindling, say. I can put myself in a position where *it* is absolutely bound to happen — though it isn't possible to say beforehand *how* it will happen, or *what* will happen.

Getting ideas and having a clear purpose is primarily an energetic phenomenon. It doesn't all happen in the mind — it goes beyond that. The mind is basically a switching station for the elements of sense perception. Working with the body means working with the mind; most often, the mental work is just the tip of the iceberg of what's going on energetically. Doing yoga and doing what's right for the body is part of being a responsible steward of one's energy. I happen to be me in this moment, by way of appearances, by the way elements perform of their own accord.

Try as I might to produce ideas at will, all I can do is be curious and organize the thinking that's present to me at any given moment. It has become important to live each day as a seeker, going beyond the concept of truth, and living the inquiry. Rather than expecting inspiration to come to me, imagining that good ideas are somehow scarce, I do things that support my practice energetically. In yogic terms, this effort means fighting the battle of *prana* (aliveness) and *apana* (dullness, heaviness). It means having familiarity with the tools and fundamentals of my practice. And something always emerges.

# A POETIC
# PROSE

> ◢ *Which one of us in his moments of ambition has not dreamed of the miracle of a poetic prose, musical, without rhythm and without rhyme, supple enough and jarring enough to adapt itself to the lyrical movements of the soul, the undulations of reverie, the turns of consciousness?*
>
> — CHARLES BAUDELAIRE

It is freeing to imagine that poetry can live in and amid words and phrases regardless of the author's intention. When I read *Moby-Dick*, I respond to the poetry of the lines, even though I am sometimes aware that *Moby-Dick* was not written in the shape of a poem. *Moby-Dick* rises from the page as poetry when I welcome poetry not as a form (such as a sonnet or a sestina), but as what arises, figuratively, out of language.

The poetry I find depends on factors that give rise to the experience. One particular phrase or form will be striking to me at one or more moments in time. What remains consistent is language's lithe ability to meet me where I am.

In the United States, the prose poetry tradition can be traced back to Europe; it can be traced back to China as well. In France, some admirable early adopters were Francis Ponge, Henri Michaux, Max Jacob, Jean Follain, and Charles Baudelaire. In China, the tradition of wen fu has Su Tung-p'o as an early adopter. The prose poem tends to be short — from a few sentences to a couple of pages — and can be referred to as a smoke-long story for the reason of duration — the experience lasts about as long as it takes to have a smoke. This quickness is an aid to perceiving the work in a way that connects to the sudden images of the dream-mind.

I am concerned that, as writers, we lean on the novel's superiority when we could benefit from looking into other forms of storytelling, other uses of language, both older and newer than the novel. A prose poetry practice leads to better novels, because familiarity with other ways of shaping experience gives writers the freedom to work more lucidly in the mode that best suits their intent. A sentence is a story; sometimes a single turned phrase can impart the very best of stories. We are only beginning to shed light on the myriad ways of shaping stories.

My approach to writing prioritizes the lucidly lived truth of the creative moment above the insistence of a polished final product. How can I know how to polish something that is emergent? I can't fully recognize what the final product will be while I'm at work on it, intimate with the experience, not holding back, fully engaged with what might be beyond my level of skill. Keeping balanced arithmetic along the way may be useful as a means of imaginative play but it won't get me there. I will get there by the grace of creativity, which transcends my intention and rewards my effort.

# SINCERITY

As I write these words, it is early spring on the East Coast of the United States. Outside my window, cherry and plum blossom trees are in bloom. Some women walk by wearing breezy dresses, and one or two of them smile as they pass a group of guys headed to the basketball court. Sometimes circumstances afford me the recognition that I am participating in a sublime interconnected web of life, in which the most amazing event imaginable has already occurred: I have somehow become a human being — and I am alive and free.

The common definition of poetry has come to refer to a typewritten thing that lives in books. These literary creations are poetry, but so is my heartbeat: its activity, its sensation, the fact that it is there. Life is the magnum opus of consciousness. Writing things down offers an organic expression of the creative moment.

To some extent, I make my world what it is. I direct my attention to thoughts and objects, my actions shape various effects. This is true and only partly true. I also exist within a living system. In a grand sense, the universe moves as one in its own turning phrase, and it's pretty wonderful that I am included in that. Because we're all in this life together, we would do well to dedicate ourselves to what makes us fully alive.

It may be useful here to distinguish the literary thing as a "poem" and the lived thing as "poetry." What is even a writer to make of either of these? I am apt to be critical, because I wonder what poetry is supposed to be doing. Poetry does not seem to put dinner on the table or drive the kids to school, though I must remember that a lack of usefulness is not always a bad thing. It's more that my insistence on getting by in the world and being useful is really part of the hang-up. Is life as a whole designed to be useful? From what or whose standpoint?

Art's job is to remind us that life is a dream, to rouse us into the experience of being. The more I give myself to my practice, the more confounded I am with wonder at how life already seems to be doing this feat that art accomplishes. Whether I willingly and creatively devote myself to a life of humanity depends on whether I am sensitive enough to the truth of my being. Whether I devote myself sincerely or not, what emerges could not have been anticipated.

> ◣ *The next real literary "rebels" in this country might well emerge as some weird bunch of anti-rebels, born oglers who dare somehow to back away from ironic watching, who have the childish gall actually to endorse and instantiate single-entendre principles. Who treat of plain old untrendy human troubles and emotions in U.S. life with reverence and conviction. Who eschew self-consciousness and hip fatigue. These anti-rebels would be outdated, of course, before they even started. Dead on the page. Too sincere. Clearly repressed. Backward, quaint, naive, anachronistic. Maybe that'll be the point. Maybe that's why they'll be the next real rebels. Real rebels, as far as I can see, risk disapproval. The old postmodern insurgents risked the gasp and squeal: shock, disgust, outrage, censorship, accusations of socialism, anarchism, nihilism. Today's risks are different. The new rebels might be artists willing to risk the yawn, the rolled eyes, the cool smile, the nudged ribs, the parody of gifted ironists, the "Oh how banal." To risk accusations of sentimentality, melo-drama. Of overcredulity. Of softness. Of willingness to be suckered by a world of lurkers and starers who fear gaze and ridicule above imprisonment without law. Who knows.*
>
> — DAVID FOSTER WALLACE, "E Unibus Pluram*: Television and U.S. Fiction"*

# WRITING AS A CONTINUAL PRACTICE

**A**s a tribe, creative people are nearly always also obsessive people. That's as it should be. It takes commitment to develop skill and to produce a solid body of work. It's not easy to unwind the authenticity that has been spooled up by years of conditioning. And to stay unwound — that is another challenge.

Producing works, performing, rehearsing, reading, writing — these things keep the wheel turning. The show is not over when one piece is finished. Years ago, at an art opening where he had some paintings, Robert Motherwell overheard a man talking about his work, telling his friend that they looked like something his eight-year-old child could do. Motherwell replied, "Yes! But day after day after day?" An eight-year-old may make such marks, but he would not in truth find that effort to be his place of practice.

It's good when I can work my creative practice into my daily life. This union in itself requires innovative thinking. The challenges of writing do not start and stop at the page. Finding place and energy and focus are more of an issue than I happily admit. There is, of course, the standby belief that because I'm passionate about something, I make time for it. Let's just start by saying that yes, this is true.

If I think of writing as a kind of performance, and I want to write a novel, then everything that happens each step along the way — even when it doesn't show in the product — is part of the overall performance, and therefore is important for me as a writer. The ritual of writing is part of me. In fact, I may discover that what I deeply wanted wasn't a novel, necessarily — it was to be a writer. I will end up finishing the novel, at which point I will discover that the work of the writer is not over. What I really needed to do all along was *be,* which means that I do not wait for a result; I live moment by moment in the truest expression of who I am.

> ◢ *Expression is when you're at one with nothingness, and you breathe with your playing.*
>
> — JOHN FRUSCIANTE

I am a writer not because I have a nametag attached to my ego that declares me a writer, but because writing, in one form or another, is natural for me. Nothing would alter that truth unless the outward form of my natural calling changed so that, for example, it evolved into what looked like painting or photography but felt the same as writing once did. No rule fixes anyone to a prescribed category. This notion of result is something that gets set aside when I really follow my path. Going beyond categories might make it harder to make sense of the world, but that's as it should be. Life invites and rewards my awe-struck curiosity.

There is monkishness to living fully. It is necessary to put aside the need to have anything else in my life except my art. Life, like art, lacks an implicit stated-from-the outside purpose. I can communicate significance, but meaning and purpose I can only enact individually, and it's my responsibility to live a life of immense gratitude for that ability.

## HUNTING MAGIC

One theory about ancient cave paintings is that they were a type of hunting magic, whereby the artist formed the images to make hunting more successful. I know there is magic to them, but I am not sure it is functional in that way.

My concern is with an argument that presumes art submits to the stomach of society. The deepest urge to sing doesn't arise to drop coins in the parking meter. Many of the painted images in cave paintings — wild horses, for example — do not represent primary sources of wild game. If I insist that the paintings were made for a reason that I deem superstitious, I am likely to believe that art is superstitious — meaning that practical living knows something of which art isn't aware. The reason for making cave paintings is no different than the reason we are moved to live creatively nowadays. I don't fully know about the hunting magic of cave paintings unless I, too, am engaged in making art. And then I know. I have a say over whether I open my creative tap. It leads me to an enticing three-way collaboration among what interests me, what there is a place for, and where my natural skills lie.

In Wolfram von Eschenbach's story of the quest for the holy grail, the hero, Parzival, at last comes upon the grail castle not through the force of his own will, and not by any map, but by allowing his horse to lead him there. As is the case with the archetype of the hero, Parzival begins his life's quest as the fool and succeeds not by his knightly training, not through his worldly conditioning, but through the volition of his innate nature in the midst of everything else. The metaphor of the horse serves well as a symbol of the subconscious. Questing wholeheartedly, I create, and what I express may carry my signature — yet is, in truth, part of something that does not begin or end when I do. Seeing writing as a practice makes me more attentive to that higher and deeper truth moving through all things.

Devotion to a practice makes me take responsibility for self-realization, which means I can no longer claim that realization is limited to me by external factors. By numbing out and closing off to what nature calls me to express, I suffer — and I produce more suffering in the world. I really need to surrender to the inner call to be wholly alive in what is truly my practice and not be limited by the outward form of that practice.

The grail castle only appears to those whom it deems worthy, and the rule is that the castle will only appear a single time. Yet Parzival was a guest in the grail castle twice. The first time, he failed at the quest, because he obeyed his social conditioning rather than the call of his innate nature. The castle appeared to him again — but he was not acting as the same person he was before. The second time, he succeeded at the quest, because he was not attached to the nonaction that was socially encouraged. Compassion moved him.

A similar paradigm shift can be found in a story from the Zen tradition known as the Ten Bull Woodcuts, which is told in verse accompanied by ten woodcut illustrations. The main character is on a quest to tame a bull (the mind). Originally, and for a long time, the story was told using only seven woodcuts. The story concluded at the seventh image, where the bull is subdued and brought back to the monk's house in the wilderness, where he meditates in tranquility. Then the tradition changed, and it became clear that there was a larger story to tell. The larger story was not finished at the conquest — more needed to be overcome. So, three frames were added after the old ending, and the story arc changed. The new story ends with a return to society. Thus, our perception of what constitutes true resolution was enlarged. It could have concluded earlier, but the larger story — the one that transcends the self — hadn't been told.

# BEING WITH THE AUDIENCE

> ◢ *In meditative art, the artist embodies the viewer as well as the creator of the works... there is a sense of total confidence. Our message is simply one of appreciating the nature of things as they are and expressing it without any struggle of thoughts and fears. We give up aggression, both toward ourselves, that we have to make a special effort to impress people, and toward others, that we can put something over on them. Genuine art — dharma art — is simply the activity of nonaggression.*
>
> — CHOGYAM TRUNGPA

**C**reation is a continual act; I can look outside and see it. Plants grow and change form, seasons come and pass, and change brings new activity. Nature continually bears fruit. Looking within, I see the same nature that I see on the outside. At the moment of recognition, I am drawn to taking responsibility for creative action. Am I breathing life into my highest truth? Every act is a potentially artful one. Just what constitutes art is open to debate, and the debate, undertaken courageously and sincerely, makes art more resonant.

I face a page in every moment. Even filling the page with words, I find that more can be written. I can look at creation in one sense and see that I have no alternative. I am here; nature is as it is. The fullest experience requires that I come to terms with that. I experience freedom only in taking action toward liberation. Picking up the pen does not require self-conscious thought. A life of inevitable meditation is the artistic path. In a Romantic sense, we are all artists. What emerges could not have been known before the moment of expression. It is fresh, and nothing will ever be the same again.

I listened to a recording of Lead Belly playing "Little Liza Jane." In the recording, Lead Belly was informed that someone had recently made a record of that very song. Lead Belly's response was "No, not like that." I never tracked down the recording spoken of by the interviewer. I didn't need to hear it to be able to agree with Lead Belly.

Years ago when I was a student, I was working late in a ceramics class. Just the custodian and I were in the studio. I was applying some glaze to a bowl I had made. I placed the bowl onto a shelf to await firing in the kiln. Several other bowls were on the shelf. Our assignment had been to make a bowl of a certain size. I was looking at the others and mine when the custodian approached. He answered my thought: "I see a lot of students here working and wondering whether their piece looks different than all the rest. They're all unique — I appreciate seeing any of these pieces on display. They're all unique and carry the artist's signature because they made it — even when they try to do the assignment perfectly and make it exactly according to design, it really is their own."

So much for the idea that everything has already been done. The custodian was right. Even without trying, I have a unique style, and the more sensitively I follow my interests, the more that style gets brought out. The painter Marty Avrett said, "Any time you sit down to do something, it may be the most important thing you've ever done." Having that awareness opens me to a wider truth. Each new thing that I write might be the most important thing I've ever done. Also, it may not end up being so important after all, and that, too, is freeing. Acknowledging that I can't know the result in advance, it's my responsibility to pay attention, get loose, and have fun.

Frustration, worry, anxiety, and judgment all have to take the back seat. There's no getting anywhere when judgment is at the forefront. I can only judge a thing after it's made. When I try and judge in advance, I prevent free-flowing expression. Maybe it will end up for the best — maybe it won't. Often it will exceed the wildest abilities of my own judgment, and all that's left is to witness with appreciation and curiosity something well beyond myself.

Judgment, criticism, and anger will never actually go away, but I can relegate them to their proper place. When I do that, these motives reveal that they are actually powerful tools. Judgment in the back seat means that as I'm writing and creating, I listen to maybe 3% of my internal critic and no more. The critical part of me is watching, and may desire to be the driver, but that desire to be the driver simply creates more energy for witnessing the actual moment of creation. If — for some reason — I'm headed for a ravine, the critic speaks so loudly that I will be able to take that into account even at only 3% volume. What the critic competes with is the still, small voice.

It's good to think about whom I am writing to, whom I am writing for — but it's also valuable to remember that I am simply writing. Sometimes I am talking precisely through the letters at the ends of my fingertips, and sometimes I am all wagging tongue and funny voice. Within the precise moment, I more or less consciously give shape to thoughts and feelings and lay them out on the page. They're there, recorded in a form that is durable and can be read later — and, through being read, experienced anew.

We've come a long way since stone tablets. Still, writing is a durable record of the shape of thoughts. Even the thoughts we think and the manner in which we record them can be artful. Nothing is better than being devoted to unbounded realization, giving form to that loyalty in writing and in life.

## UNCONSTRAINT

Great writing begins with movements of the mind and hand, unconstrained by style, form, or even expectation, unburdened by self-representation or importance. Because the creative moment is unconditioned, I can't know what will be represented, but I should trust that when I am heartfelt, the work will express the moment's truth.

When I embody the unconstrained writer, spontaneously and upon revision, I trust the reader, trust the process, trust the brain's ability to form useful patterns. As the unconstrained writer, I trust my heart's ability to express, to transcend the perceived limitations of form or function. Unburdened writing is prolific writing.

The transformation into unconstraint takes faith. I get better as a writer by employing useful criticism. I need to know what to make of the material I produce. But, first, there must be enough material to survive critique. The goal is to produce enlivened, energetic, original, creative work. It's good to envision perfection not as the absence of flaws but as the presence of something original.

The emotions propel and sustain me far better than the intellect does. It's more valuable to improve the best parts of work than to focus on parts that aren't working, better to try something strange and interesting than to dwell on preconceived notions of what defines a successful piece of writing.

> *The important thing is to believe in what you're doing, even if it's absurd. Most people's rational consciousness prevents them from doing what they should have blind faith about.*
>
> —— ED RUSCHA

I am told time and time again that writing is hard work. Of course writing can be very hard work, but it will never be the same as digging ditches. Ideally, the challenges of writing don't feel like a burden. It is best when any work — whether ditch digging or phrase turning — is so fulfilling that I am compelled to work hard at it.

My editorial ego usually wants to assert itself by deleting material, or preventing the material from ever being written. As a writer, there is really no sense in letting my internal editor have its way. Instead, I remember that the editorial or critical ego is potentially the greatest service to the creative impulse. My drive to criticize can ultimately lead me to being my most productive; in fact, the work I produce can only get better when the impulse to create is informed and guided by my internal critic. The critic wants to have fun, and the creator wants to be directed to where the stakes are high.

During creation, the primary force at work is the chaotic, the uncontainable. Its opposite, the formed, the boundaried, the conscious, is most admirable when it is not believed to be the final truth. I have within my capable reach the force of the sublime domain of madness and music.

> ◢ *All writers… have had some philosophy, some criticism of their art; and it has often been this philosophy, or this criticism, that has evoked their most startling inspiration, calling into outer life some portion of the divine life, or of the buried reality, which could alone extinguish in the emotions what their philosophy or their criticism would extinguish in the intellect.*

— W. B. Yeats

I begin writing by writing without remembering what makes a piece of writing. I write so that the pages pile up and structure is born of its own accord. There's not always a good reason why a written piece needs to look a certain way or adopt given dimensions.

When I decided that I was going to write twenty books in a year, I made a list of what I thought would be good titles for each book. As a way of getting started, I daydreamed some way of framing each book's experience. It wasn't too tricky to come up with the first ten or so titles. Beyond that, I really had to think about it. And because I came up with twenty rather than just ten, I came to look at each book in a different way. I had to try out several different modes of writing and of organization. In my better moments, I had nothing to prove.

Poetry happens — and it happens when filing taxes, when dreaming of warfare, when writing, whether or not it takes the outward form of poetry, and it happens when reading, because poetry is a relationship between subject and object, the shape of thoughts and feelings. I don't have to add or color it to be any other way.

# APPROACH
# VERSUS FORM

> ◢ *Meditation in the MIDST of action is a billion times superior to meditation in stillness.*
>
> — HAKUIN EKAKU

The exercises in this book are meant to help writers produce work they are happy with, in life and on the page. Think of them as yoga practice. The purpose of what happens on the yoga mat is the experience of greater union with the divine through the body. It is an expression with inward significance. Yoga and writing should both be looked at as offerings.

Writing that has been treasured for centuries and passed down might be spiritual in nature, ecstatic, entertaining, instructional, or even bawdy recordings from real human beings, written so long ago that they seem too important to have been put together by human hands. Looking closely at the collected writing where authorship can be traced, I see plenty of so-so or off-putting pieces mixed in with what's good and celebrated.

Good writing, enlivened writing, writing that I enjoy stems from engagement with ordinary experience. It is meditation in the midst of action. I write about whatever I like. I let the form happen; I let the feeling dictate the structure my writing takes. I let success happen and don't let anything constrain my relationship with the imagination. It's hard enough to stay on the path where creativity deepens and thrives over the long term.

I write from life when that strikes me as significant, and I write imaginatively when that's what I feel called to do. When life is filled with pain, I strive so that my work heals and transcends that pain. Energetically, when it disrupts the expected flow of events, pain can shake things loose in a way that leaves me more liberated and empowered. When my life is lucky and happy, I am authentic to that lived truth in my writing — I share the depth and specificity of that; the one who listens to my words as I put them on the page wants to feel my efforts to make a sounding board of the soul. Whatever my circumstances at any given moment, I have the opportunity to direct my thoughts toward an all-encompassing compassion, and in this way, practice yoga. Moments that could potentially be most transformative are often not easy. The more I practice, the more the momentum of practice carries me forward.

Practice means to focus on my life's work of peace and love with regard to the kind of creative pursuit that takes me for the full ride, the most challenging trip imaginable, and the one for which I alone am uniquely suited. The result of transcending the ego is benefiting others. This is something we all can do.

This approach connects me with the natural world. It is meditation in the midst of action.

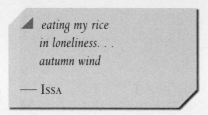

eating my rice
in loneliness. . .
autumn wind

— Issa

I think of Hatha yoga as poetry of the body. Yoga is conflated with its physical appearance. Poetry is conflated with its literary appearance. Yoga and poetry might just be the very same thing. Goethe said that everything is a metaphor — and all metaphors mean more than one thing. A garden in summer is the warm hearth in winter. The barista leans forward to whisper something difficult to discern and is the oracle of Delphi.

My twenty-book year was productive, but being productive in itself is not the best thing in the world. What matters is whether I am relating authentically to my craft, whether the articulation challenges me — and whether I am unattached. Sometimes I get flummoxed about publication when the best thing would be to create work that stems from my immediate experience as an offering to my social sphere. It is beneficial to work with equal integrity whether there is widespread distribution or not.

My advice: Write something that exceeds your abilities. Strive to offer the world something that blooms from effort and disposition in a way for which you cannot accept credit. The imagination, not the ego, is worth celebrating.

I wouldn't say that writing as yoga practice is a replacement for other forms of yoga. My writing may be the most important thing for me to do, but I benefit from meditation. Hatha yoga practice was designed to be the fast track to experiencing true freedom and enlightenment. I benefit from doing good in the world. I benefit from living sustainably.

My practice speaks to the importance of bringing the light of consciousness into places of pain and awkwardness. When doing so, parts of me relax that I didn't even realize were constricted, because it's habitual to have kinks and hang-ups. Interior work helps me maintain my new habit of being open. I direct my attention toward objects that connect me to gratitude and amazement. I let these thoughts magnify my love and my means of giving form to that love. I don't let comparisons interfere in a negative way. At this point in time, I don't think that cynicism is any damn good for anything.

I had been meaning to watch the movie *The Secret Life of Plants* for several years, but just never sat down and watched it. I found the film's concept fascinating, and I enjoyed Stevie Wonder's far-out soundtrack. So, eventually my wife and I watched it. I was emotionally and spiritually moved by the film, by the beautiful time-lapse photography, by how it celebrated a close look at growing things. I loved to see the various scientific findings (whether they were really scientific or not) because they expressed an intuitive truth. Whether someone actually was able to teach her cactus to speak Japanese (one of the film's claims) wasn't as important as the richness of attention given to living, growing plants. If plants were able to communicate with us in our language, we would recognize that they — like us — are not simple quantities of mass. Our own life is something we understand (at least in theory, if not always in practice) to be precious and wonderful and rare. The film was more than a little sad, because it projected such hope for the future, and it was already thirty-five-years old by the time I watched it. I admired the film as a piece of poetry that forgivably clung literally to what is, instead, a figurative truth.

I put faith in science. I value when science is able to demonstrate something. In many ways, I value science above intuition. But often, I hope that science is able to demonstrate something that may just not fall under a perfectly rational purview. If I like something, I might not want to bother trying to demonstrate scientifically why I like it; I just like it, and that's how it is — for the time being. Someone might be able to demonstrate relationships between my behavior and the action that I claim to like, or between elevated brain hormones and increased circulation when I am exposed to a given stimulus; perhaps that link would illustrate arousal, though it hasn't really dealt with the concern of why I like it. At the moment of my death, science won't save me — nor will science give me comfort.

Living and dying are more art than science; because something is an art does not make it "soft." Conformism comes from dependence on what has already been proven. It benefits me to allow room for curiosity and wonder in my actions. Where the practice of poetry takes me is the only place worth going.

# SPEAKING WITH EYES CLOSED

**N**ot very long ago, an accident damaged my eyesight, and the doctor told me that without surgery, I would go blind in a very short time. He said that in both eyes, my retinas were peeling off. As a result, vitreous fluid would leak into places it wasn't supposed to, and the retina would continue to undrape — like faulty wallpaper — so that light entering into the eye would be refracted uselessly. It would be lights out, and before long, the eyes, too, would rot and need to be surgically removed.

I had seven retinal tears in my left eye and nine in my right eye. A couple of days after the news, I underwent surgery to repair both eyes. Part of the recovery required that I spend over six weeks lying on my left side with my head tilted at a forty-five-degree angle. Three months and several in-office procedures later, I was finally allowed to do things that were remotely strenuous. I was finally permitted to bend over to pick something up. Prior to the surgery, I had been very active and physically fit. Being still and seeing the body lose its vibrancy and tone wasn't fun. I had a lot of trust in my doctor. I remained as positive as I could and tried to be productive. I had a lot of time to reflect on life.

During the time I was recovering, I listened to dozens of books on tape, including *War and Peace*, a long book, and with the help of some patience and my then-fiancée, Jade, I planned our wedding and marketed our first Wellness and Writing Immersion Retreats in Italy. There was so much in life I couldn't do, so I focused on what I could do. I wouldn't describe the experience as a meditative one — it was more like a dream. The way the mind gives pictures when dreaming happened all the time, which made listening to audio books a vivid and complete experience. I think the state of being near a dream facilitated new ideas and allowed concepts about writing and about life to sink in.

I was more introspective during those months of recovery because I felt that I had to be. I couldn't really see, so I couldn't adjust what I was saying to fit the listener's visual cues; I had to speak from the heart or not at all. Keeping this internal frame of reference has been important for me. I cannot control what other people think or feel, but I can manage my own thoughts and feelings.

Dinesh Bahl, the ophthalmologist whose expert abilities prevented me from going blind, is a wonderful human being beyond his skill as a doctor. About a year after he repaired my vision, he got engaged, and just prior to the wedding ceremony, he learned he had cancer. Though his operation went well and his prognosis was positive, the experience affected him. I went to see him for an office visit because I wanted to say hello, and found him a changed man. He told me that his wedding was the best day of his life, even though the operation prevented him from speaking his wedding vows aloud. "There's more to life than work," he said. This is the man whose work prevents people from going blind, and he meant it, and it's true. We promised to keep in touch, and I know he meant that, too.

If this person, whose job is to prevent blindness and restore sight, deserves to take time for himself, then we can live fully for ourselves no matter our vocation. Being able to give someone your true smile from deep down is no small thing. We should welcome each twist and new development insofar as we are able.

# SHAPED WITH QUICKNESS

> ◢ *Among Chuang-tzu's many skills, he was an expert draftsman.*
> *The king asked him to draw a crab. Chuang-tzu replied that he needed five*
> *years, a country house, and twelve servants.*
> *Five years later the drawing was still not begun.*
> *"I need another five years," said Chuang-tzu.*
> *The king granted them.*
> *At the end of these ten years, Chuang-tzu took up his brush and, in an*
> *instant, with a single stroke, he drew a crab, the most perfect crab ever seen.*
>
> — *from* ITALO CALVINO'S *Six Memos for the Next Millennium*

It was a wise king who granted all that was necessary to Chuang-tzu. I like how Italo Calvino introduces his essay on "quickness" in works of literature, because his example highlights the wisdom that everything along the path to attainment can be understood as necessary. Chuang-tzu *needed* another five years, just as he needed the servants and the country house. Even if a writing session doesn't produce any material you'll *use*, you may find that you needed to do it.

Yet, one might ask: What did they do, these required elements? They may not have been directly functional, yet they are far from being extraneous, and instead factor into the totality of the artist's lived experience. Whether my work is representational, I work from life —from lived sensual experience. Honoring the energy of what is immediately before us is the most sustainable fuel for our ability to imagine.

I am reminded of an anecdote about Pablo Picasso: Picasso was having a few drinks with friends in a bar, let's say, and an art collector approached and asked Picasso to make him a painting. The art collector was so happy to have crossed paths with Picasso, now late in his career and exceedingly popular. He was desperate to have something from the master, so the collector offered a lot of money for an original piece. Agreeing to the offer, Picasso took out a pencil, scribbled on his napkin, and handed it to the collector. The collector was disappointed and told Picasso that it wasn't fair, that he had spent no time deliberating over this scribble. Picasso promptly responded that it had taken him fifty years to draw that piece. And it had. It took fifty years of experience to arrive at a place where he was able to render it and to recognize that what he had done was, indeed, a piece.

Whether intentional or not, whether a mistake or a success, each step is an expression that blooms into the eventual result. How I respond to each creative step forms the character of my work. It makes for a better result now, and it builds toward better results in the future. This process is true despite the doubt that arises in the moment, which wants to limit the results to those fitting into a preunderstood category. Vying for conscious control, I may gain the ability to explain and defend my actions, but I shortcut creativity. Authentic creative confidence acknowledges the blessing of being drenched in a spacious mystery.

When we honor the moments in our creative flow that have the most charge and intensity, the resulting work can be said to move with quickness, because the reader senses that the work is alive and growing. Quickness rewards the reader's trust in the written experience as an imaginative one.

In other words, each nuance and detail, each turn and departure, can be trusted as necessary, even when the details are nonfunctional in a structural sense. Isn't life the same? Isn't it a matter of perspective whether a detail becomes significant? Because not everything can be decided properly in advance, I find it fruitful to focus on how I can add onto the pieces rather than remove them when they don't seem to add up.

Let's say that in writing a story, I discover that I have landed on the image of a certain Colonel Sanders on the side of a bucket of Kentucky Fried Chicken with more energy than I would want to understand. Then the energy departs. Follow the writing elsewhere, and what will likely come up is the transition from a single image (Colonel Sanders) into repeated images or figures that show contrast without necessarily structuring the story. There may be a similarly registering passage with an imprint of a bespectacled, goateed cartoon devil, thus making clear what you had been getting at with the image of Colonel Sanders. Even without textually linking the two, my reader will likely feel the possibility of the two existing as metaphors of something parallel and uninvoked.

Although a departure into unknown territory is confusing or uncomfortable for me as a writer, the return reassures my reader. When I follow an author through an elaboration or departure, I am often better able to enjoy it when I know that the author is true to the way things arise and is being "quick," as Calvino uses the term. It ends up building trust.

Wildness in creative practice honors the moments in life that feel the most full. Sometimes when these imagined bits don't connect to anything essential within the story, they encourage the reader to feel the most alive, whether the departures are haunting, wonderful, or both.

# A LIFE OF CONSCIOUS MAKING WITH NOTHING EXCLUDED

**T**he artist, the poet, and the yogi are aligned in their aims; only the outward form of the practice is different. A phrase turns, and it turns us, turning a wheel in the afterimage of creation. In the moment of turning, we glimpse the one. Through action based in the wisdom of devotion, I come to see the self in all things; and, through seeing the self in all things, I am compelled through compassion to act spontaneously, with nothing to prove.

We should never be too certain of our legacy — if J. R. R. Tolkien had been overly emphatic that he was a linguist and nothing besides, he'd never have let himself spend so much time writing *The Lord of the Rings* — and it surely must have taken a lot of time.

As artists, we want to make our lives into the real dream-within-the-dream of functional existence — the reverie of the flow of everything. Life's story ends at death — and life's stories get told by those of us who have no other perspective. The best we have is a story in a story. Because the story can never be complete, we should strive for sufficiency.

> ◢ *Knowing that nothing need be done is the place from which we begin to move.*
> — GARY SNYDER

I have a strong reaction to my associations with the word "sufficiency." It has a lot to do with my experience with the Zen tradition of Japan and with being in nature. Lately, going through old photographs to use in a book project, I've been remembering a time many years ago when I was studying at Cape Breton University in Nova Scotia, where the campus itself was out in the woods between two towns. It was winter, it was cold, and it snowed a fair amount. The campus at night, especially just after a snow, was an astoundingly quiet and peaceful place. To go for a walk through the deep, dark woods, all I had to do was head south for two minutes. I would go for a walk every night as it snowed — often not until two in the morning. I dressed in several layers and headed into the trees. Where there was a recognizable path, I would head elsewhere. When there was no wind, there were only the sounds of snow. A dead tree would moan as it leaned. Cloudy overhead, no moon, it was nearly impossible to see. There was almost nothing — but the overwhelming sense of being alive. The silence and dark and cold, the familiarity of trees, the feeling of being isolated and even lost — these feelings starkly contrasted with the stimulus of daily life. The present moment felt wholly sufficient.

I feel a huge relief and a sense of wonder when something clicks into place as "enough." For example, Issa's haiku:

> the way things are —
> through my worthless window
> days grow longer

The simple declaration registers as much bigger than the space it's given on the page. Time seems to have slowed. I can't be sure it hasn't.

> looking at me
> the pheasant on tiptoe
> on tiptoe

This second poem is a lovely example of pausing for a moment with an image, and working that image so that it stretches larger in time. The pheasant on tiptoe isn't enough. It needs to be

>     ... on tiptoe
> on tiptoe

# EXERCISE: EXPAND THE ASYMMETRICAL

A common example of symmetry in a short story is beginning and ending with the same (or very similar) movements. A fairytale might begin with "A long time ago, in the clouds, at a time when things were grand," and end "happily — oh, so happily ever after," the hero surrounded with admirers departing back into the story's mist.

This same symmetry happens in a typical five-paragraph essay, where the information in the introductory paragraph is revisited when it's time to conclude the essay. To some extent, we enjoy symmetry, because it affirms our sense of things, provides a model for reducing complex issues, and guides us through the cerebral "in" and "out" doors. Yet we aren't poetically satisfied because the work itself isn't satisfied, because life is not truly symmetrical. No writer is more skilled in this regard than Kevin McIlvoy, whose prose resounds with waves of energetic asymmetry that invites the reader into the spacious and disorienting moment-of-telling. We want writing to share the asymmetry of life. If, instead, the writer asserts that everything turns back to normal at the end, we feel haunted by the suppressed subconscious, knowing that something has changed.

The asymmetrical presents an opportunity to expand the parts that stick out. As an exercise for a piece you have already written, draw out these asymmetrical moments so that they highlight a significant image or action. Introduce something dissonant to interact simultaneously, and then be playful as you figure out what happens when the two scenes affect each other.

Here is an example in summary form, with inserted dissonant scenes shown in *italics*:

A couple is showing their new house to their friends. They have just explored the basement. One of the friends, twirling her own house key on her finger, lingers behind to check out their collection of whisky.

*A cat has entered the basement and starts playing on top of a piece of paper with a rubber band.*

The friend, holding an extremely rare bottle of Scotch whisky, gets distracted. Her attention is captured by the cat's excited pawing.

*The rubber band gets lodged underneath the white sheet of paper, and the cat feels on top of the paper, knowing that the rubber band is there, but can't see or smell it.*

The host, now upstairs, says the phrase "water of life," which is what whisky means in Gaelic, and the friend hurriedly returns the bottle to its place, and all is well, except that she has also left behind her own house key...

This exercise works to create new, layered, dynamic scenes, because it gets us to focus playfully on how things in life are always out of balance. Through the interplay of parallel scenes, even if one thing is resolved, another more significant thing becomes unresolved.

We are charmed by the attention given to unraveling, and we want to be given more than the prescribed constraints of storytelling. We want to feel the imagined world acting on this world not as something that could exist as a summary. We don't want the "right" story. We want the living story that is fresh and original. The living story adjusts to the listener, to the telling, and is based on the circumstances that brought about the story being told. We want this moment to express something beyond belief, to surprise us with the interplay between structure and asymmetry.

# EXERCISE: THE WRITING MARATHON

Beyond simply putting in the time, having the kind of internal disposition where your relationship to your imagination feels intimate and sustainable is necessary to finding success in a creative practice. The most successful and prolific creative people put their creative practice first in life, because they see it as a practice, rather than a series of obstacles leading to a result, whether that result is a book, a career, or some kind of recognition.

When I see my writing as a practice first, irrespective of the result(s), I am able to tap into an inexhaustible supply of creative resources, techniques, and tools. The desire to have my efforts validated by external means can actually be the greatest barrier to growing as an artist. It's hard, because I want an audience, and I don't always get that. I try to maintain balance between having an integral practice and knowing when and what to share. The imaginative reward is first and foremost within my being. I have learned that the time is always right to become more honest with myself and to reconnect with what strongly motivates me.

Creative domains are always changing outward form. As time moves forward, each innovative project reveals more of the scope of what is possible with words. Internally, the answer to what form your writing should take is in the pursuit of your project's emotional truth.

Sometimes when writing, I feel stuck. I don't know where to go. Well, I'm not exactly stuck, though that's how it feels. Not stuck, but sticking. Often it's just that I'd rather do something else. And then something unsticks — maybe I go for a run or have a conversation or find something to drink that changes my state of mind — and I'm in the flow again, and it feels good.

It's nice when a change of setting or headspace gets me unstuck, but it's best to unstick myself without needing to phone my friend or play bocce or bass guitar. The way to practice is by doing a writing marathon; it raises my personal investment in the project by devoting a large chunk of time and working continually without looking back.

The writing marathon is a way of writing for an extended period of time without stopping. Whether I begin with a project in mind or head into the thing with no conscious expectations, the writing marathon is a powerful experience.

The writing marathon is a practice in integrity, asking that I grow more curious about my writing. Rather than adopting a fixed idea of what my project can be, and editing it down to that, I remind myself that it's a gift, and not one bestowed exclusively to whom I think I am. My writing gets better, because I establish a close relationship with the imagination and because I want to employ myself in creation.

For getting unstuck, the most important thing to remember is that *I want to write*, and so I keep a positive outlook. As I write, I mediate my focus among things, characters, settings, dialogue, on myself, on asking questions — and on answering them. I experiment with wording and especially with phrasing. When

I've been writing short sentences, I write a longer one. This exercise gives my brain other things to focus on besides the writing. The experience becomes more dimensional because I am directing my attention toward facets of the writing process other than those that come naturally for me. I rove, finding freshness in each moment's succession of images. More correctly, after-imagery is most present to me.

Images — whether perceived with the senses or with the mind — remain in the vision after they are seen. I'm sitting in the window seat on an airplane, and I've just woken up from a brief and unrestful nap. I'm curious what time of day it is, so I draw up the window shade to find that the sun is bright and very orange on the horizon, above a thick mattress of white clouds. It's too intense; it's painful. I shut the blinds and look away. My eyes re-adjust to the dark of the cabin, but there's still a disc in my field of vision from looking at the sun. That's the sun's negative after-image. The photoreceptors in my eyes have been overstimulated. Though I'm looking at something else entirely, I can't help but see that peculiar energetic shadow left by the sun. Eventually, it fades, but the basic mechanism for after-imagery continues.

The brain trains itself to simplify things, to make order of disorder, and to ignore what seems unimportant. I experience the world, I grow familiar with what it feels like to do certain things. I sit in a chair, and before long I'm not really conscious of the fact that I'm sitting on a chair. This works well for me, for the most part. Otherwise it would be difficult to get anything done. It helps, though, to constantly bring more craft nuances into my field of attention. I work to become more aware of the fact of language, the sound of it, and also to the feel of speech, of the tongue's movement, where the sounds resonate in the physical body, and whether subtle patterns exist in all of this.

When I detect patterns, I have something to toy with, to think about, something that can be manipulated and experimented with. I often begin a scene in a given way, by first providing the context, then a description of the general environment; this process seems traditional to me. I'd like to mix things up. I could keep the general descriptions to a minimum, and instead look to a specific object to impart the feeling of the place and establish character as well. Perhaps my characters are in an environment with strong verticals — a peculiar upscale hotel lobby. Instead of beginning with a description of the lobby, I could describe a minor character's penmanship — the strong verticals and dramatic crossed Ts of his script. Moving forward with this pattern, I feel more like exploring the space, and I notice that someone passing through the lobby wears her hat tilted in a mock-dramatic way, and it complements her walk — a too-upright strut.

If need be, I forget that I am writing — on the verge of the other world — and do my best to pass on through. As with the above example, I could describe the linear architecture of moods. The story will still get written if I stretch my attention elsewhere periodically, and it's a good exercise anyway, because I'm pouring thought and care into it.

I can't help but be inventive when I'm really paying attention. Wasn't it that way all the time as a child? I may get rusty with this ongoing creativity but I don't ever fully lose it. As the years of childhood passed, I set aside childish inventiveness, because I become more concerned with appearing normal and being successful with other people. After all, I need to belong, and I want my contributions to be well received. But I put too much faith in the rewards of appearing normal and being successful, and I miss out on how inherently joyful it is to be authentically creative.

The primary means of re-energizing the writing process is to explore innovative organization, progression, and structure. This study helps you overcome the main challenge of the writing process, which is staying meaningfully in the flow of imagination.

The best and most enduring core concept is to be mindful of images and to track things as the images reverberate with me and in the work. I modulate my focus to bring variety and play into my style, remaining continually attentive to the moments with the most energy, in which I — as the writer — feel peculiarly charged and flickering with strangeness. Particularly in those moments, I am aware of the imagery at work. When the moment passes, what remains? Can I re-elicit a gesture that harkens back in some way?

A great thing to do if I begin to lose track of things is to restate, in a kind of summary form, what happened in a previous passage that was working particularly well. It's a big help in longer writing marathons to help keep track of where I've been and to re-sound moments that felt striking.

If I feel blocked, I can reiterate the most recent phrase I have in mind, altering something about the phrase with each repetition. This reiteration is an exercise in overcoming the limiting belief that I need to stop in the middle of my writing. I've led many people through session after session of writing marathon, and it has been a positive experience for everyone, and each writer has been able to do it. My first writing marathon went for a full twenty-four hours. If I can do that, anything is possible.

The writing marathon is not exactly stream-of-consciousness writing, because the intent is not to capture a steady stream. I can organize my work in whatever way feels right for me. I enjoy the clarity that comes from working modularly, roving from section to section, if need be. If my thought skips to a new topic, I leave myself some white space to signal that. The writing marathon is not automatic writing, because automatic writing is unguided writing. The writing marathon is a delving style of free writing, where I write persistently for an especially long period, taking responsibility for shifts of nuance and focus — managing free play and direction, growing more conscious of the writing process, of myself, and of generating enlivened, unburdened creative material.

I do no revising. When in doubt, I review, retouch, or resound. Each time something happens, it is spontaneous. The moment of creation is garden-fresh.

## RULES AND REGULATIONS

**Regulation I: (Duration)** — Write for the duration, by long-hand or on whatever device you'd like.

**Regulation II: (Rate)** — Write/type at the rate of one letter per second or faster. This rate is the required minimum, not a required mean that would be calculated over the entire time period. (Plod; don't write for a burst and then rest.)

**Regulation III: (Breaks)** — Take a fifteen-minute break every three hours. Get up and move around. Then return 100% to your writing.

**Regulation IV: (Continuity)** — Don't look back and reread what was written. Don't be concerned with quality. Do, however, focus on having fun.

It's OK if I eventually discard the vast majority of what I write. There's no rulebook that says good writers keep everything they've written. There is no permanent record of all my drafts. Doing Hatha yoga, I don't get to keep the postures I've performed. In writing, I continually try new things and experiment. If I am not writing at all, I won't have anything to show, so I have fun writing. It's an extension of who I am.

I need ground beneath my feet. I like the feeling of being right, of having ideas click together, of making meaning, forming patterns, and feeling practical. Paradoxically, more than that, I need to rise above that ground. I need variety and the chaotic potential that goes with it. Just as I need to know things for sure, I also want to venture forth into the darkness. I want surprise.

Change itself only takes an instant. Habits take time. On average, most people take about four weeks to adapt to a new habit so that it feels natural. Until that fourth week, the new action may seem unnatural and uncomfortable. After a while, though, any attempt to change from that new habit would feel even more uncomfortable.

I look at the regular practice of writing marathons as a method for opening into a new expression of who I deeply am.

# ACCOUNTABILITY
## <u>EXERCISE</u>

- Send a message to your friends to let them know when you are planning a writing marathon. Tell them how long it will be.
- Post another message to notify them when you have finished your marathon.

Accountability is a big motivator. Plus, if your friends are writers, your writing marathon encourages them to start their own. If at all possible, doing writing marathons as a group in the same room helps. Everyone can be working on his or her own project, silently sharing in the energy of being productive.

The writing marathon gets you to make a lot of written material without censoring or artificially shaping the natural voice. It is a method that invites in the irrational mind to play without incurring criticism. There may be no surer method for writing with access to prelingual resourcefulness. However, if you would like to pause — to create chapters, to change sections, to read where you have been to see that you are on the right track, to sketch out where you would like to go so that you will be able to return to an outline of good ideas if you become less inspired later — you are free to take the liberties that best suit your creativity.

# 2. TANTRA FOR WRITERS

# WHAT'S WITH THE TIGHT HAMSTRINGS?

**W**riting is foremost a mental experience, but it's inevitably a physical one as well.

From an outward appearance, the writer's kind of physical activity usually involves hunching over a notebook while seated in a chair. Sustaining this position can afford substantial benefit, because language has a powerful effect on the way I think and feel. It also leaves me with tight hamstrings and a stiff neck.

My experience as a writer and yoga practitioner has taught me that the physical practice of Hatha yoga and the thought-based practice of writing are closely related. Conscious communication stretches me, expands my perspective, and sheds new light.

The term *yoga,* as it is commonly used, signifies a category of physical stretches and postures. Thus, on a retreat in Bali I might say that I am on my way to "do yoga," meaning that I will be performing various postures on a mat. The Sanskrit word *yoga* refers to a practice that readies the mind for wisdom and actually means "yoke" or "union." So, if I want to practice yoga in that sense, I practice union. Metaphorically, I can practice that kind of yoga through writing.

Hatha yoga is a physical and spiritual practice. The word *Hatha* refers to a balance between the body's polar extremes: the cool, rational head (the moon) and the fiery passions of the pelvis (the sun).

Central to yoga is the belief that mind and body are one. It is immensely helpful to have language to guide my thinking. Without the affirming guidance of language, my thoughts are left to their own devices. Words can support me, and words help translate what I'm feeling into substance for meditation.

Self-talk, that on-the-spot writing on the mental chalkboard, has a powerful effect on my physical body. When I'm holding my eyes closed while standing in tree posture, my brain is flooded with stimuli from my nerves. It's a storm. Wind seems to be blowing my branches in all directions. The longer I hold the pose, the more overwhelmed my mind feels. What do I say to myself to keep balanced, to fully witness the sensation and allow it all to flow, evenly observed, neither praised nor rejected? How to hold difficult postures — not out of force of will but out of devotion?

I stand in tree posture, feeling rooted, finding stability. Making the minute adjustments that keep me standing — the adjustments at my ankle, the arch of my foot, my leg and hip, my core, the swaying of my shoulders and arms — am I adjusting to the wind? Do external forces shift my stability? Or, is the wind and fluctuation coming from within? Is it a physical phenomenon

— are my muscles learning their dimensions — or is it a cognitive phenomenon — am I adjusting to the unsteadiness of the storms of thought?

I draw my attention away from the search for stability and stretch into the rootedness I feel in the moment. As I stretch, I open my senses to feel more of the elements that flow through me. I imagine how much a tree with a hundred leaves feels the sunlight, and how a tree with ten thousand leaves feels the sunlight on each leaf. Everything that surrounds what I can feel is consciousness; the sunlight and blue sky are alive between the branches.

Yoga teaches me that I am a work in progress. Some self-improvement takes care of itself by going through postures with sensitivity and correct alignment. When releasing a yoga posture, I simply feel good — no thought required. As I become more familiar with the postures, the sensations are not "new" anymore — the same is true with language and vocabulary. I tend to say the same things to myself. Inevitably, the subconscious mind churns up challenging issues on the road to self-knowledge. Sometimes when moving through the same yoga postures, I feel lousy, perhaps even afraid, because a physical sensation threatens my self-concept. It is vital to make distinctions between the postures and language that serves me and stretch away from that which doesn't.

The Sanskrit word *asana*, taken to mean "seat," is the term for the yoga postures that I do. Yet, wonderfully, *asana* can also be understood in a more general sense as one's place in the world. These distinctions are important because yoga practice trains the mind as well as the body. Becoming obsessed with how I look when holding warrior posture will affect my conduct in the world. Language yoga helps to direct my attention inside.

Even when yoga begins as a fitness practice, it is hard not to discover that it is a spiritual practice. Within a posture, emotions arise. Beliefs and feelings get stored in the body, and clinging to those that don't serve the greater good drains my energy. Yoga frees me to become more fully myself, which entails going through moments of negative capability. When practiced as a manifestation of union with the boundless imagination in the present moment, writing is a form of yoga.

My own introduction to yoga was a gradual one, and to be honest I looked into just about everything else before really moving forward with yoga. I began with the Christian Bible, then onto an interest in indigenous religion. I read books about Zen. I read about Mahayana, and I read the Dhammapada. For years, I looked into the Tibetan practice of Tantra and was particularly drawn to Dzogchen.

I only really came to understand the spiritual tradition of Hatha yoga when my wife and I attended an intense teacher training on the Hatha Yoga Pradipika taught by Yoganand Michael Carroll at Jacci Reynold's studio in Santa Fe, New Mexico. That class changed everything for me. No longer could I think of yoga as a sequence of stretches. Yoga can look like that, but it's deeper. Hatha yoga is an intense path toward realization. It has had a powerful effect on my writing.

# TANTRA

The Yogic tradition holds the concept of Tantra. Most people have heard of Tantra in conjunction with sex, as in tantric sex, with the understanding that it's a kind of sex that is spiritual and lasts a long time. Tantra can be translated as many things, and is perhaps most accurately translated into English as continual, stretched through, or weaving. The tantric practitioner's practice does not start and stop on a yoga mat. Instead, the world is my yoga mat. The practice of Tantra, therefore, never lets me off the hook.

The alternative is to live and die with my song still inside. Tantric practice brings awareness into every activity and moment of my life. As a result, I experience union of mind and body, self and other. Witnessing myself connected to other beings naturally leads to feelings of loving kindness and *ahimsa,* or nonharming.

As a writer, I find this practice immensely helpful, because of the challenges I face when putting words onto the page. Writing challenges my sense of self, because only sometimes is it as simple as merely putting words — symbols and letter combinations — onto the page. I am exposing a vulnerable part of myself. Writing as a tantric yoga practice gets me to renounce my expectations. What emerges, I discover, is a truth of sorts, natural, as I am natural. My writing is most triumphantly natural when I pull out all the stops — both of self-criticism and of discipline — and perform as myself, openly, ongoingly, right now. In practice, this effort requires a kind of meditative work that does not begin and end at my intention; rather, all is an inevitable meditation.

I doubt, rationally, that I perform optimally, and so I prejudge — that is, based on a kind of aggressive fear, I try to prevent myself from acting. This struggle doesn't work, because trying not to act is itself a kind of action. Fear asserts that the present-moment articulation is insufficient. When I widen the flow of focus to the present moment, am fully attentive, activated and viscerally engaged, the world is open before me. I lose myself in the flow of craft. It becomes a wonder that words are not merely clumsy symbols after all.

Practicing even a little bit of Tantra is very good. Because life in general is an offering, my own life is best lived as an offering. The page is an opportunity to express and perform, no different than the moment before being confronted with the page. All that matters is that writers bring the truth of their entire being to bear in the performance of their words. Rather than being something difficult, the challenge of being true to myself is a task for which I am perfectly suited. Having the intention to write, I simply begin as I am, following a path set for me that I am gifted with the awareness to experience as it happens. Sometimes I would very much like to know where it all is headed, but that insight is just not for me to know until the moment is upon me.

Tantra Hatha yoga practice has three main practicable facets: *asana*, postures, the way one is in the world; *pranayama*, breathwork, the way one works with *prana* or aliveness; and *dhyana*, contemplation (traditionally, seated meditation that the body was made ready for through asana practice). It may be significant to note that when the practice of dhyana was brought to China, it was called Ch'an, and when it made its way to Japan, it became known as Zen.

Tantra Hatha yoga was originally practiced as the fast way to self-realization. Monks would follow very specific guidelines interpreted by their guru (the hope is, correctly) from their experience and the *Hatha Yoga Pradipika*, build a small hut in the woods, and practice full time, having set aside the material world, except for what was necessary for them to practice.

The way yoga was practiced by the ancients is very different from the yoga commonly practiced in studios nowadays. For one thing, it was solitary. Without any self-conscious social expectations, the experience was more introspective. Yogis went into the woods to discover who they were, devoid of any context. Renouncing everything, practicing yoga, yogis came to know the natural self.

I practice something similar as a writer, and as artists, we have the path before us. Life in the woods at Walden Pond changed Henry David Thoreau's life in a yogic way. I can live each day more monkishly by freeing myself of preconceived notions about what the finished product looks like — whether that's a particular kind of success, precision about where my work is headed, or a way of being received. I let go of these things, because when I cling to them, I'm not free to live to the utmost, as I am. This freedom allows the road to success to contain at least some measure of fulfillment each step of the way.

True Tantra Hatha yoga is exclusively for those who have renounced the world, and contains no code of worldly conduct. Those practicing yoga who still live in the world would follow a different path, such as the one put forth by Patanjali, often called the Eight Limbs of Yoga, in which the external world is not taken to be illusory. The renunciate's path is strictly internal.

Language is a wonderful medium for yoga practice, because the act of writing is one of sustained attention, and writing creates a record of how I present my thoughts as words and phrases.

# IMAGE AND RESONANCE: HOW POETRY IS FELT

> ◢ *Poetry appears as a phenomenon of freedom.... A man's work stands out from life to such an extent that life cannot explain it. Art, then, is an increase of life, a sort of competition of surprises that stimulates our consciousness and keeps it from becoming somnolent.*
>
> —— GASTON BACHELARD

The reverberation of an image is its felt effect on the surrounding language. Reading, listening, writing, or thinking, as I move from image to image, word to word, each symbol uniquely affects me, and these effects are colored by my experience and the surrounding language. Life is the context of resonance.

In tantric yoga, the word *nada* refers to the unstruck sound. In nature, all sounds are produced as the effect of two things striking or rubbing together. To experience *laya*, or dissolving into oneness, nada yogis direct attention to the constant sound of the inner ear.

The word *poetry*, insofar as it stems from the ancient Greek verb meaning "to make," signals a kind of attention that can make things that give the reader an experience of true being.

Image precludes meaning. Resonance conveys individuation. Image resonance is a lens, a clear lens, through which attention is paid, as the stuff of life flows into supportive and musical structures.

*Sound* as a verb becomes personal because it always resounds *with* and *against*. Within the undulations of oneness is individuation. The represented image is the true lie and the shape of truth.

A significant image reopens to my awareness that I am living, and that it is living. A significant image unites noun and verb at the moment of emergence — such as "I am," for example, or "God loves."

# MEDITATION EXERCISE: YONI MUDRA

*Hear no evil, speak no evil, see no evil.*

You have seen the three monkeys that embody this phrase: Sitting side by side, the first monkey with covered eyes, the second with covered ears, and the third with covered mouth. The image of the three monkeys carries symbolic insight — that we have an animal nature. We might think of this animal nature as the energetic, uncontrollable monkey mind, ruled by the need to satisfy the senses.

The antidote to a mind tethered to unstable senses is directing attention into the depth of one's nature. Within the mind, beyond all sensation, is the source of instinct. Paying close attention, we tune into the truth of which our cells are aware. The peace of attentiveness opens into the bliss of being.

We see metaphors for the self-liberating force of instinct at play in the animal world. Baby turtles hatching on a beach know which way to go to find the ocean. Within moments of hatching, they head straight for the rolling, crashing waves. As a first sight, this — their only path — must look daunting. Yet, the turtle's instinct is that beyond the churning of the waves lies their true home. You won't find a sea turtle just giving up and trying to make a living on land. Though it may not look tempting to the turtles, the sea draws them by instinct. Following this path, the turtle sees life on land as a thing of the past — and the land dissolves.

Because living true to your deepest nature requires overcoming the desire to placate the mind with sensations, we imagine alternatives, and so another story is useful here. I have heard of a simple yet effective trap used in some parts of the world to catch monkeys. Hunters put roasted chickpeas — which monkeys love — inside a hollow coconut, and then they wedge that coconut underneath a large stone. The coconut has a hole in it just large enough to fit the monkey's hand through. In theory, a monkey can simply stick its hand into the coconut and take the roasted chickpeas. However, the holes aren't large enough for the monkey's clenched fist to exit, thus the coconut forms an effective trap and an elegant symbol for attachment. Even a smart monkey will not want to let go (after all, as the logic goes, who would want to let go of a sure thing?), and all the hunter has to do is walk over and grab the monkey.

We use logic to justify our position, even in the act of tethering the self to a snare. As a result, we can hold liberation in our hands without being able to enjoy it. It is wonderful to know that meditation can be a path to achieving liberation. Whether liberation manifests in life as greater freedom of emotion, a more relaxed mind, or more ethical conduct, meditation frees us into higher modes of experiencing everyday life.

Below are two techniques that offer an opportunity to enliven your internal awareness.

# TWO TECHNIQUES

## 1. Ujjayi Breathing: The Sound of the Ocean Inside

To breathe making the ujjayi sound, move the glottis as you would when whispering or when relaxed in deep sleep. This narrowing of the breath's passageway produces an oceanic sound that is extremely useful for bringing the attention inside during meditation and asana practice. The effects are made more dramatic when closing the eyes and ears, as when performing yoni mudra.

## 2. Yoni Mudra: Closing the Sense Gates

> *After his practice develops and progresses he gradually hears subtle and more subtle nada. In the beginning of practice loud sounds like the roar of waves, rumble of thunder, big drums and trumpets are heard. In the last stage subtle sounds that are latent in the body like the jingling of ornaments and the sound of a harp and reverberation like the humming of bees come within the range of hearing.*
>
> — HATHA YOGA PRADIPIKA, *Verse 84-86*

The thumbs are placed over the entrance to the ears, the index and middle fingers are placed lightly over the eyes, and the middle and pinky fingers are placed over the mouth.

Optional: Yoni mudra with kumbaka (voluntary cessation of breathing). Position the hands as described above, with the ring fingers pressed against the nostrils on either side, temporarily closing off passageways of breath at the point of inhalation/exhalation.

# PRACTICE

To perform yoni mudra in meditation posture, seat yourself on a small cushion or rolled-up towel so that the abdominal muscles do not need to exert any work to hold your torso tall.

Be sure that you are breathing into the whole range of fullness in your chest cavity: the abdomen, the middle chest, and the upper chest. To test the fullness of your breath, be attentive to the extension of your belly, the expansion of your ribcage, and the slight raising of your clavicle.

Position the hands into yoni mudra, paying particular attention to the sound of the closed-off ears. You will notice that, in this position, you can be acutely in tune with the slight movements and repositioning of the arms through the vibrations heard through the tip of the thumb.

With equal attention, begin making the ujjayi sound during the in-breath and out-breath. Hear the sound of the ocean inside and dissolve into the infinitely varied, distractionless tranquility.

# VISUALIZATION

*Breathing in, be beneath the flowing waves of the ocean.*
*Breathing out, be above the waves churning against the shore.*
*Inhaling, pull into the endless flow of the sea.*
*Exhaling, emerge from beneath the waves onto the surface.*

# EFFECTS

This meditation, which combines yoni mudra and the ujjayi breathing, is a powerful addition to any introspective practice. Whether you predominantly practice yoga asanas or seated meditation, this meditation is an excellent addition to deepen your practice. It brings the attention inward and demonstrates the overwhelming richness of the internal sense environment, which is very helpful for encouraging a more regular practice.

## SUGGESTION FOR GROUP PRACTICE

Solo meditation is recommended for those seeking to develop introspection in an independent fashion; however, group yoga and meditation are wonderful opportunities for sharing the positive vibes of a group dynamic. For maximum effect, the following positioning is encouraged.

Each meditator sits on his or her cushion in a circle facing away from the center of the circle. For introspection, it is psychologically beneficial to have the group energy confirmed at your back, with each meditator facing outward, like the radiating warmth of the sun's rays.

When the meditation feels complete, the teacher/facilitator signals the conclusion to the students by touching them lightly on the head or shoulder. The students, with eyes still closed, release from yoni mudra and relax their hands to their waist, feeling the tranquil quiet of the self at rest, contrasted with the memory of the churning energies inside.

# NADA YOGA AND
# RESONANCE

◢ *Eternity is in love with the productions of time.*

— WILLIAM BLAKE

Normally, when something gets bumped, nudged, knocked, or hit, it makes its sound, and that sound is not a pure tone. Instead, the sound is a mix of several different tones, and thus is classed as predominantly percussive rather than musical. Then there are objects, like chimes, that ring and ring, the note continuing at a steady volume. After the moment of sounding, the object vibrates in unison, and the sound produced is clear.

At some point in the process, the ringing object comes into itself. There is a sharp volume curve after the bell, tube, or bowl is struck, or the string is plucked, and then the object has a bit of time for the sound to reach the extent of its dimensions — and the sound, having traveled the sum, revisits the source.

For a tightly drawn string, I can measure its pitch. How tightly is the string drawn? How wide is the string, and what is it made of? Then, what is the string fastened to, and what are its characteristics? In the case of a guitar, what is the wood? How has the wood been shaped? And, how does the shape of this object interact with the surrounding air?

Production of sound is one thing — the ticking and clicking of insect legs — and resonance is another. In a quiet room, I'm able to hear the grasshopper taking bites from a leaf, because the leaf is constructed so that it readily rings forth with its paper bag rain patter notes, even as it's being munched. And, in that resonance, I am made to feel.

It also happens that I feel things that haven't produced the physical ringing of a bell, yet are metaphorically or symbolically striking. This resonance happened to me earlier this morning as I read a haiku written by a friend and former retreat participant Bill Dollear:

> Old acquaintances
> Flee from my circle of life
> Like melted snowflakes.

Writing the haiku, Bill did not actually strike a bell, though I reacted to his haiku as if he had. I told him that I was struck by his lines. The way he wrote them produced a kind of reaction that I could only refer to as resonance. Good writing has the capacity to be present in such a striking way that when a reader comes to experience it, the language resonates with him.

Good writing doesn't require a reader to be successful — it is simply present, and directs presence toward openness. It exists in eternal space, where it is possible to create a response that is fresh no matter how much time has passed, unique based on the reader and the circumstances that have brought him or her to the moment of witnessing the play of language. Writing is unique each time it is read. Reading and rereading create different experiences.

The repetition in good writing shows its living structure; musical patterning connects me to the way I live each day. There is a fair amount of repetitive action in ordinary life. Yet, there's no way to sum up experience — it simply has to be felt. And, being felt, where attention is heightened to experience the immediate moment, each movement and encounter will not be felt as truly repetitive. Nothing in nature ever repeats itself. I grasp the concept of repetition, and I can find repetitive actions, but when truly present to the repetitive thing, I find that each iteration is unique. The linear model of experience passing through time is helpful but sometimes incomplete — perhaps it would serve me better to feel that experience blooms and unfolds as time moves forward. And while I can find comfort and order in a cyclical model of recurrence — such as the movement of the sun giving rise to the recurrence of days and years — no day is ever the same, no New Year's celebration is ever the same. I pass familiar geography, but I do so from a different perspective. Each moment changes everything — how could it not?

I return to the contemplation of sound produced by natural objects, remembering another class of sonic production that I haven't mentioned: the flute. Rather than being as obvious as two objects striking each other and one producing its sound, a flute-type instrument makes its note through the friction of air; provided that the air is blown at a particular speed and volume, the flute will resonate. Brass instruments are similar, and make their sound from a resonance that follows a buzzing sound. With the resonance of musical instruments comes an increase of sound. But resonance as a whole occurs in minute ways as well. The grain of wood affects the flow of resonance through a harp. The shape of an ear, and how it is positioned relative to a tone, affects the shape of the tone that gets picked up. I'm describing a tone as something with the quality of shape because of the perception that even within a pure tone, a clear note, there are discernible characteristics, and the characteristics I notice depend on many factors. A straight-on tone is open to more of the full spectrum. An ear facing somewhat away from a sound hears more of its reflections, both from the environment and the ear itself. In this way, even a pure note is perhaps understood as "only" characteristics, without a single part uncolored by circumstances. Even in the silence of the earth turning on its axis, I am present to all sound.

When I hear something beautiful, something that resonates with me, I open myself to that experience. I may want to turn the volume up, and I will also want to clear more within myself, sensorily and attentionally, to more fully witness it. To the extent that I'm able, I strive to become a better sounding board to that experience. Resonance naturally carries an emotional quality.

There is an even more mesmerizing class of sound body: the object that resonates with sound. The crystal glass that breaks when a pure — let's say piercing — note is sounded. The glass's characteristics have imparted their own pitch, let's say a particular nuance of oscillation within the vibratory frequency of the note A. Not a perfect A, but a little sharp. When that vibration resonates with the glass, the glass, too, sounds, and perhaps because the glass is not perfectly constructed, an exterior, powerful tone overwhelms its construction, and it bursts. Of course, tone resonance is not always visibly destructive. It may be thought of as a kind of magnetism — for awhile, the vibrations effect the object, and it rings back against the vibrations. Play a tone against a standing fluid such as water, and you can see the wavelength of the sine wave. Such is also the mechanism of poetry and of any emergent form. It transcends structure and support.

# WALKING TRUE IMAGES

> ◢ *When a man makes a poem, makes it, mind you, he takes words as he finds them interrelated about him and composes them — without distortion which would mar their exact significances — into an intense expression of his perceptions and ardors that they may constitute a revelation in the speech that he uses.*
>
> — WILLIAM CARLOS WILLIAMS

In communication, we use images. The image as imparted by me is a relation between the thing and you, halfway between the expression and the audience. There is no exact science to the use of images. The chief talent is adoration.

When I am true to myself, I find that that's what the world really needs. If I'm communicating in a way that isn't in line with my will, my voice — to speak contorted against who I really am — I won't be as fulfilled, and the image won't have as much staying power or as much effectiveness in the real sense.

No truth is permanent and lasting, because all truth gets expressed by something. It is wonderful that everything expresses some truth. Language serves to direct attention, and postures direct attention as well. Slouching in a chair both limits the thoughts I can have and encourages me to have other thoughts. Standing on one's head has the same affect, but toward a different end. Both are right. More than what I think is happening is happening.

When I no longer cling to anything else, I still have myself — as I really am. When the mind and body are not insisting on separation, doing what it is my will to do becomes easier. The way I phrase things creates effects in the world within me. Words are the sense elements of the mind. Therefore it is best that practice is pointed to the place from which metaphors come. Stepping into the shoes of negative capability, I experience creativity and wonder. To achieve an outcome, I don't even need an agenda if I have the discipline of practice.

I am only me for a short time. I may think I own the house, but I don't own it forever. I get to be a steward of energy. The world is created as a sacrifice — not at pains, necessarily — but as an act of transcending the self. I must act, and the only way to be free is to act naturally.

Entering the moment, I find a new expression, different than what I came expecting. What I need is never exactly what I think I need. When I try and hold on to what comforts me, I don't grow. Are my personal goals really what I find myself dedicated to sleeping and waking? I live most fully when directing my attention toward the eternal in the present moment. It's marvelous that I get to be the experiencer at all. Potentially, everything could be blissful. The challenge is being open for it. I try to remember this when showering outdoors at my cabin, and there is no hot water; when a breeze rolls in, I remember: *It could be blissful.*

Releasing an arrow from the bow, I do what I can and trust the rest. After I release, it's someone else's job. All I can control is my body, my posture, and the angle of release. Once it's gone, I have no say over where it goes. I like to think that I do, and I keep watching it closely, maybe trying to steer it one way or the other. Trying, I squint, I lean, and I grimace.

As purpose filled as I can be with my life, something is going on that I shouldn't ignore: I am a newborn and mother nature is very large, very old. I can make the best of what I have, but I can't make it permanent. Knowing limitations is actually a great gift of freedom. Self-realization is my main task. To get there requires renunciation, the kind that gets you to enter the world again, so that you depart even from the sacred space of practice.

What appears like success or failure may, in time, turn out to be the opposite, and with more time may appear of little consequence. If I feel like a failure, I do things that justify feeling like a failure. If I feel like a success, I do things that justify that success. So, in the moment, I seek sufficiency and gratitude in the middle way between living and reading, and I produce material that is enlivening, directs presence toward openness, and creates surprising clarity. Listening for music stretches my ability to hear.

# FREE OF STORY: A HISTORY OF BOUNDLESS LOVE

◀ *It does not matter whether there is liberation or not — surrendering to the divine energy brings unbroken happiness.*

— HATHA YOGA PRADIPIKA, VERSE 78

Long ago, prior to Tantra, the school of Sankya was prevalent in India. The practitioner of Sankya understood there to be five senses, plus the mind. These senses are never without an object. The mind's object is language (or images). Each sense has its respective objects, and the senses are only experienced in relation to an object — there being no way to taste tasting or see seeing, as such.

The Sankya practitioner believed that only the self was real. Every object in the universe consisted of elements, and Sankya practice helped to detach the self from sensory experience (via discrimination). The practitioner was on a quest to detach from all sense objects, which is one way to be free of the drama of life. The ego is hard at work to negotiate suitable places for us amid the drama that begins with the senses and their objects.

Imagine that I walk into a teashop, and I notice two people sitting at a table talking to each other. I have dated both of these people in the past. They're talking to each other. That sight would give me a strong charge. I could see only the component parts — two people sitting at a table. Dating is just a word. The table is wood with metal screws, and the people, in turn, consist of various elements. The goal, in this case, is not to do anything, but rather to eliminate all charge from worldly concerns.

This practice is useful but problematic if something is more real than the self. Also a problem: It is not possible to go about life without taking any actions. Tantric yoga expanded from the paradigm of Sankya and taught nonaction in action, or action without attachment to the fruit of one's labors. Through this practice, one relinquishes the ego and invites the higher self as the doer. This practice is messy particularly when it is not a solitary practice, because the potential for distortion grows when many egos are involved, when many stories converge and compete.

Tantra practice asks that I relinquish all ego concern and let the boundless nature of love manifest through my actions. Delusion or suffering is an outcome of conditioning. When I relax and free myself from my conditioning, I act more in line with my true potential. Achieving greater freedom is an intimidating process; body and mind cling to what's familiar.

The Sanskrit word for the ego is *ahamkara* (self-shape). Ego is hierarchically superior to the senses and the mind. The ego manages the mind and body to move toward thoughts and sensations that affirm it — and away from those that threaten it.

Carl Jung taught that, at a fundamental level, all human beings inherit the same images, the same charged stories. In the Hindu text the Mahabharata, and specifically in the *Bhagavad Gita*[1], we encounter representation of the ego in the character Dhritarashtra, whose name means "to cling tightly." Dhritarashtra is a blind king whose army in the *Bhagavad Gita* is fighting against the hero Arjuna. It is key to remember that the ego is blind — it cannot see what is best for it. When it clings tightly, the ego does not serve its best interests as a ruler.

When the ego battle is fought, the persona in the place of the ego is not Dhritarashtra, but Arjuna, whose archery skills enable him to acquire something as-yet beyond him. Even more remarkable is what happens at the end of the battle, when Arjuna recognizes that he never did the killing — a shadowy form always struck before he had been able to act. To recognize the superiority of this shadowy form is the function of the internal witness or knower (*buddhi*), which is superior to the ego.

The more I come to identify not as the ego but as the witness, the more I move toward self-liberation. The ego does not really possess the independence it asserts. Thus, the Zen master Dogen said that "Mountains and rivers of themselves become wise persons and sages."

The internal witness grants wisdom and discerns truth. I open the ego to *buddhi* through meditation, contemplation, and concentration. Hatha yoga is a kind of battle that helps make the mind/body ready to practice meditation. Practice makes the ego

---

[1] I highly recommend reading Winthrop Sargeant's version of the *Bhagavad Gita*.

into a friend. That we have the sense of self is, in fact, an unfathomable gift. When we no longer cling to keep it out of fear, we are most soaked in awe.

The awe is magnified as we come to understand that something exists beyond the witness. Superior to *buddhi* is something twofold: *prakriti*, unbounded wild nature and all material manifestation, found always in union with *purusha*, the consciousness imbued in nature. *Prakriti/purusha* differs from *buddhi* in that *buddhi* is still attached to a self, whereas *prakriti/purusha* is impartial, infinite naked awareness. Truly diving into totality, inheriting everything, we are the most haunted because the self has no shape to which to cling.

Tantra is an ongoing internal and external practice. Rather than looking to external means for achieving satisfaction in life, fighting for success and control, Tantra grants perspective to the flow of existence. Grounded in the understanding that my desires are not the final answer, I learn my boundaries and benefit from counsel. I become a whole individual, satisfied in myself. Deeper into the practice, moved by wild nature and unconditioned awareness, I am moved by love to act freely with integrity.

Through this hierarchy, I can understand in fundamental terms how my component parts are not separate from the elements of the natural world. Expanding the sense of that oneness, parts of the self relax, parts of the self grow — all the while the universe expresses itself. I don't think so much about myself or about what I write than about what is truly here — and, in that relationship, I seek and express clarity about the nature beyond me. The search for truth, the high pure of it, gets in the way.

# EXERCISE: EXPAND SUFFICIENCY

As writers, we sometimes make mistakes. It's true. Sometimes we overthink and overexplain the significance of an image that the reader may be apt to celebrate if only we knew when to leave well enough alone.

A trick is to know when to highlight the image and when to leave it to the reader to confront the significance. We want to avoid being heavy-handed, so we avoid overexplaining. We want to avoid being dramatic, so we tuck away significant images into the structure of a work.

Look for twenty opportunities in your written piece to honor the sufficiency of the incomplete, the mysterious. Rather than leaving the image alone, and without leading up to it, see if you can give the reader more time. Can you repeat a phrase? Can you enlarge the reader's sense of the thing by describing a nuance or element within the thing? Can you invoke the image again in a different order? Can you create a pause through syntax or punctuation? Can you make a mistake as a storyteller that tells a truth (as when leaving an issue unresolved, redirecting focus toward something else)? As long as readers know the written piece as a whole is going somewhere, and the pace is agreeable, they will delight that you are able to expand their sense of time, as they confront details that could otherwise be dismissed.

# 3. MODES OF ORGANIZATION

# THE
# LISTENER

Everyone has a different experience of the same text. When a group of friends reads a book and gets together to talk about it later, each person will have a different opinion of the story's plot, its significance, and the best moments within the story. Each, truly, will have a different perception of the story. The reader experiences the written creation extended into the new moment. I may have someone in mind whom I'd like to have as a reader, though I can never fully know how someone will receive my work. Each reader is unique, each moment of reading is exceptional, and the way each reader comes to the work is distinctive.

My projection of the reader affects the way I write. I think of this immediate presence as the listener — the figure on the other side of my immediate efforts. The reader finds the work later — sometimes a great deal later — after the initial experience has passed and new experiences have arisen.

It is useful for me to have an idea of what my psyche is projecting upon my writing. At any given moment, the listener will change, and this change mirrors my own subconscious movements. The listener serves as a guide for me to take the path through language that merges with the desires of the work. This voiceless spirit is the truest guide.

# CHOOSING A BODY

> The old red blood and stainless gentility of great poets will be proved by their unconstraint. A heroic person walks at ease through and out of that custom or precedent or authority that suits him not. Of the traits of the brotherhood of writers savans musicians inventors and artists, nothing is finer than silent defiance advancing from new free forms.
>
> — WALT WHITMAN

In putting words down on the page, language moves from the realm of the imagination and acquires a body. The words become a piece — a collection of signs and sounds that has accrued shape in the mind of the listener. I picture grape vines growing on a trellis. Given time and a bit of training, the grape vines will add to the structure, and they will strain it. I might feel that they work against it, although that is not their intention. The intent of words and vines is to live and grow with blind faith. I prioritize language's capacity for emergence, and am at the service of its wanton meandering. My primary focus is to guide and utilize supportive structure in service of what wants to arise. Language's vines are trained and coaxed to grow in the way that best serves the drinker of wine.

This model of literary structure is at play in the world as well. Society's gridded structure is most sane in the service of nature. Solar panels are a prime example of this dynamic. I could wander up and down mountain trails as much as I want — I won't come across a solar panel that has naturally grown out of the ground or has been cast down from the limb of a tree like a pinecone. The supportive structure of industrial society makes this construction possible. Choosing to structure my life in service of nature brings me to live in a cabin in the woods with an array of solar panels, benefitting from our ability to direct the supportive structure of industry and technology to serve the wider net of interconnected life.

In much the same way that we see the aimlessness of urban development, we would do well to remember that a supportive structure is not superior simply because it is load bearing. Cities are not better than wilderness. Each is as it is. All the while, life arises within and without structure, in the quality of light on the cabin's beams, in the characteristics of its wood grain, and in the moisture, fungus, and heat of erosion. I am at the command of living structures whether I know it or not.

The world has many examples of urban sprawl — supportive structures, to be sure, but the kind of organization that is not at the behest of a beautiful aim. It is not for everyone to till the soil, and it is not for every storyteller to be a poet-monk. Yet it does behoove me to be sensitive to where my food comes from and where the life in my language is.

In my view, there are two structural models:

- Supportive structure: rhythmic, boundaried, dealing with the crystalline stability of images and themes, central characters and grounded details.
- Musical structure: lyric, dealing with intuitive progression and a sense of flow

When a scene winds tantalizingly on and on, I would say that the musical structure is dominant. The listener reacts to the music of the written word. When, on the other hand, a scene demonstrates a sturdy scaffold of organization, such as dated entries in a logbook, supportive structure is dominant. These structures are overlapping notions— whether we perceive one or the other in a work is largely intuitive.

Amid both of these structures is what arises from the work itself, its poetry, the living flame, the self-organized, the emergent. Emergence is apt to occur in any structure, but most openly when the writer's approach welcomes uncertainty.

# MUSICAL STRUCTURE

Musical structure deals with the organization of sound and resonance through time. Rolling a boulder down a hill creates noise but not music because it has not found organization. The initial impulse was triggered, and after that the boulder entered the percussive realm of natural sound — which is simply what happens when a boulder rolls downhill. At first it is active, then it becomes passive. If, instead, I had placed many boulders along a high ridge and dropped them off in a regular or ordered sequence — say, one boulder every two seconds, the resulting sound would create more total noise, but also potentially something more musical, because there has been more association. The boulders would strike against the same contours as they made their way down the hillside, and the listening brain would perceive some music because there is some intention toward association.

In writing dialogue, one experiences a musical progression; it feels right or it doesn't — I react to it, expecting the kind of flow that happens naturally when bodies relate through dialogue.

Breath follows a musical structure. Its depth and tempo and volume closely match my state of arousal. Talking and moaning and hiccupping are upsets in the conformity of breath's musical structure.

Musical structure exists in character development and inter-actions across time. Motifs and guiding imagery flesh out the supportive structure and coax the reader's hand across the story's body. The majority of fictive works consists of musical elements.

The flow of writing can rely on our felt understanding of music to learn how it propels forward. In listening to the progression of chords, one hears the sounding of two notes lean forward in anticipation of a third note to complete the triad. The structure of music is available in the natural world, but it doesn't always manifest as such without the effort of the composer to structure the sounds so that they convey harmony and discord as the piece of music desires to express them.

Things want to recur, but I will always find them different. I will change, the image will change, and through it all, music may happen. I plant several lemon trees in large clay pots along a path to a formal garden. Each morning, I walk down the path to go to work in the garden. I see the same trees every day; with each day, I have a day's worth of experience; I grow older, and at least a little bit different. The trees are qualitatively different as well. It is early spring; the trees grow. They later bloom and fill the area with fragrance. Small buds form and, from the buds, fruit will grow. Bees and insects frequent the lemon trees; the leaves move in the wind. Each night the pores of the leaves open, and they respire. In bright sun, the color of the leaves is affected; chemically, they are at work with photosynthesis. If the mind is our sixth sense, perhaps the sense of time is the seventh sense. Somehow, we sense that time is passing, perhaps perceiving the constant of time through our varying interactions with it in states of arousal.

In music, an interval is a combination of notes. The notes may be sounded at the same time, or there may be time between them. We respond to the frequencies within the note and especially we respond to ratios between the sounded frequencies. A chord may sound comforting, or peculiar, or, as is true in Balinese gamelan, there are evil intervals. In writing, I find examples of intervals at play. When there are two scenes, what links them, what separates them, and what are the dimensions of the emotional/energetic bridge between them?

When we see one scene, we may expect another particular scene to follow it. When there is a wedding, we expect a honeymoon. A story that consistently adheres to such expectations feels flat, because its music blends into the background of our expectations. If, instead, we revise a formulaic interval to what might feel like an octave of difference — raised or lowered stakes — we impel the listener to react differently. There is a double honeymoon. One honeymoon has the voice of a tuba; the other, the texture of a vibraphone. I begin with an intention — and the form isn't known until I follow the approach dictated by my ear for music.

## SUPPORTIVE STRUCTURE

Supportive structure works because it offers a system in which the work as a whole shows its independence. Think of the graph drawing of a plot arc. Recall the historical details in *War and Peace.* Think of telling a friend a joke, then explaining to her a meandering bit of backstory to help qualify why the joke is funny. The history textbook from my middle school years forms a system of self-governing chapters that make sense even when removed from the rest of the book's context. One could open up the book and begin to read about pre-Columbian North America, and it would make sense because the book's structure offers discrete sections.

Supportive structure is also hierarchical. When there is a hierarchical book, within that book are parts, each of which has sections or chapters. Each chapter, in turn, may have headings and subheadings.

Supportive structure is often networked, as in an encyclopedia or dictionary. A friend of mine and I once spent a good couple of hours exploring the ways words are related through the network of a dictionary. I recorded this effort and developed a kind of spoken word album from it. We began with a word, read the definition, and chose a word from within the definition. We then read that word's definition, and kept on going that way.

Supportive structure is often latticed, where images are stitched or woven together in an overlay for the reader to explore. More than being overly guided, the reading experience is organically encouraging. Plot level concerns interweave. Let's say the main character, a boy, searches for the lock that fits the key that he finds in a blue vase on the highest shelf of his deceased father's closet. That is his plot, but it is not solely his story. Things that other characters want alter the boy's quest and decentralize it from the main storyline. Historical information comes into play, following a latticework of narrative, expository, and imagistic threads.

# EMERGENCE

◢ *Poetry is not an intellectual exercise.*

—— GARY SNYDER

A piece of writing can have any sort of body — the key is for it to breathe. Poetry's domain is this crackling realm of association. What to do with images that do not prod the reader forward? These images emerge as life moves through the written form. Emergence frees an image of projections.

The morning of the day I married my wife, I went for a walk through the woods of Tuscany. I didn't follow a path. I came to a wild boar trail, and I followed it, passing mile marker stones measuring the distance from Siena. Parts of the trail were overgrown with tree limbs — too low for a person, but plenty of headroom for a family of boar. There was no path, let alone a main road — it had been hundreds of years since the road from Siena had come this way. I thought about how the boar had kept the path long after the highway had been diverted for flatter ground. There were squarely hewn white marble building stones but no structure anymore. I was in a valley — I slipped and tiptoed along a relatively slick path through the wash of mud from an uncommonly rainy spring. Several locals had been consoling my wife (in case our wedding day would be a rainy one) with a phrase of good fortune, something to the effect of "a wet bride is a lucky bride." The day began partly cloudy, but by noon, the sky cleared, and our wedding, out on a hilltop, was beautiful. White cows mooed in the distance.

Objects hold a charge when I am attentive to them as part of the life of the work. Decorative elements gain texture, details, shadows within shadows. This type of communication is essential, yet nonfunctional. Like being beside a flickering fire, poetry rewards the listener's openness to the experience of wonder. Poetry is the way language lives. A work is most alive when unselfconscious, feeling to be unshaped by aim and, instead, magical, discovered, reported as-is.

I am apt to confuse emergence with magic. I do not know whether magic is real or depends on the play of appearances. I do not know that I could discern the two. I am apt to lose the attention of some readers when speaking of spirits and magic; however, it's a disservice to my experience if I avoid using such terms. When in doubt, things can be taken figuratively. For me, figurative language is the most real.

Temperature and humidity form ice crystals on a pane of glass. That ice materializes into intricate patterns like snowflakes is an emergent phenomenon. It appears to be blessed beyond the fact that temperature and humidity are at work. A tornado is an emergent phenomenon. Wind is air flowing from a high pressure area to an area of lower pressure. Many who have witnessed a tornado feel that they are experiencing a thing with intentionality.

In the mountains of Big Sur, it is not uncommon for the sea breeze to carry in low-lying clouds and fog that envelop the redwood trees growing in the canyon bottoms. One minute the sky may be clear, and only a moment later, the sky far and wide around is white and opaque — the fog has rolled in. It may last for days, and it may venture off in a matter of minutes. On occasions I have witnessed something pure and magical in the motion of the fog, where white wisps detach from the herd, then wander in from the sea and, like dragons, explore the treetops and cloak the nesting birds. Irrespective of what might seem to be wind patterns, the dragon does not dissipate as a cloud might, but instead roves, rolls, and returns at last to the white horizon.

## MODE

A writer's mode refers to a wide-reaching general concern for putting together a creative project. Regardless of mode, an author can be working in the domain of poetry.

When I express from the mode of story, I am basically trying to get somewhere. I still invite poetry to reverberate in the background. The intent is to communicate in tandem with living — that is, things becoming and interacting.

The difference here between the modes of story and poetry might be expressed in the terms *life* and *living*, whereby the poetic image is imbued with the ecstasies of life, and story proceeds like veins in marble, which, traced, seem to be living. In the end, story and poetry can emerge to much the same effect through different modes.

I have a different set of expectations (or constraints, depending on how I think of them) based on what I'm doing with language. When telling a story out loud to a group of friends, I do not have to give a formal introduction. It's sufficient to begin at the thread of thought that led me to the moment where it felt necessary to tell the story. That might be an image from the middle of the story. No matter — I can rearrange the story (as it exists in my mind) in whatever way I need. The story as it gets told depends on the moment of telling — the overall mood, the receptivity of my audience, and what I particularly wanted to highlight. I often forget that everything can still be rearranged when writing a story down. It seems that I need to start at the beginning, when it's nearly always the right thing to simply begin where I first confront a vein of the narrative. To delay admitting what is immediately present to me will sand away the woodgrain of the story.

My intention is to prioritize the emergence of images as they arise from reverberation with the written material. Material that succeeds in this mode cannot be intentionally generated (or at least not for long), and can only be rendered as something emergent.

# LEARNING STRUCTURE FROM ORAL TRADITION STORIES

Several years ago, I was discussing with friends what they felt was the meaning of the word "shape," as used in creative writing workshops. I quickly learned that everyone had his or her own definition, some in opposition to others, yet this term was often thrown around when critiquing work. After much effort and some light-hearted debating, we arrived at a suitable definition. Shape refers to the reader's impression of the story's structure.

Stories from oral traditions are rich and often strange, especially when it comes to how they are structured. While the premise of many stories has to do with explaining one thing or another, in the most entertaining cases not much emphasis is placed on the explanation, and most of the story's energy exists in other elements, sometimes in things that seem to bear no effect on the story as something instructional.

Take, for example, a common type of oral tradition story: the why story. In one story there can be a storehouse of information — if the story leads directly from the proposition "why" to the outcome ("because"), the story would be lost.

"Why are roses red, grandpa?"

"Roses are red because there is a pigment in their petals."

There is an answer to a question, but the story has gone untold, and his answer offers no metaphor for living.

I asked my wife: "Why are roses red?"

She answered: "The golden sun had three daughters. Two of the daughters took the form of the night sky's darkness, and one was vivid red. The red daughter was always chased by nighthawks because she didn't blend in with her dark-night sisters. She was tormented so much that she would take stones and tie them to her slender body — the stones weighed her down to sink underground to a point below the horizon, where she could not be seen. She has been alive for a very long time, and she has borne many children. Now the shy red daughter shows her face when mother sun is out. All her children have thorns, which remind us of their independence. That is why roses are red and why night hawks never pluck them."

"Why" stories impart the richness of living more wisely than any correct answer. Oral tradition storytellers honor ideas that arise during the telling, and, if there is a way, they include — rather than exclude — the spontaneous, directly lived experience in the telling. The listener has as much to do with the story that gets told as does the storyteller.

> ◢ *People say that what we're all seeking is a meaning for life. I don't think that's what we're really seeking. I think what we're seeking is an experience of being alive, so that our life experiences on the purely physical plane will have resonance within our own innermost being and reality, so that we actually feel the rapture of being alive. That's what it's all finally about.*
>
> — JOSEPH CAMPBELL

# EXERCISE: WHY

As you write, take departures as if you were writing a why story. The truth in each why departure does not need to be literal or factual. Aim instead for a lived, enlivening truth. The occasion for your departure may be as simple as a scuff left on the wall of your protagonist's home. Once departed, be sure to reiterate. So, for example, in your first departure, you show the reader the scuff's presence and give some notion of its shape. In your second departure, you answer the question of how it was left. In your third departure, you take the reader into the moment when it gets cleaned off, yet the action that caused it is shown to affect the protagonist in that moment. Do not worry about the need to fill the page with words. Instead, permit your hands to record what you imagine. Remember: There are many voices to choose from, not just the editor's or the usual writerly voice. Ask a different question, get a different answer.

Addressing "why" concerns beckons both enjoyment and the employment of skill. When I am just beyond my expertise and comfort zone, and I am having fun, the listener relishes the experience.

I could provide an example from one of my own projects, *Pants in a Tree*, a short book-length piece that began as a light-hearted and relatively aimless project, adherent only to the device that the story would occur in repeated instances, scenes where an elderly man, the genius, comes to discover that his pants are not on him; rather, they are high in a tree, swinging in the wind. Something actually came about by sticking with this project. I needed to feel out more of the situation of the man — why he was alone, where he was, and just what sort of genius he might be. The listener for *Pants in a Tree* wanted to dwell long on details, to celebrate the otherworldly. I told the quick hints of a story by moving through a time-ordered sequence of prose poem episodes.

As it has happened, *Pants in a Tree* turned out more serious in tone and argument than an immediate introduction to the premise might suggest. There is something evocative about a scene that one finds repeating endlessly.

If I had listened to the direction of the internal teacher at the expense of being attentive to the internal fool, I would have dismissed the project as too light. On the other hand, if I had only taken the praiseful guidance of the fool, the book would not have been internally challenged enough to reveal the subtleties of the protagonist's experience.

# "THREE THINGS" EXERCISE: NONESSENTIAL ORGANIZATION

This is my favorite exercise. I used it to put together several of my book-length projects.

1. I decide roughly how many chapters I would like my book to have. If I don't know, I say thirty.

2. For each chapter, I come up with three unique images (which could be of any sense, and are not limited to the visual). I then simply imagine interesting images, ideally those that hold a charge and in some way pertain to my creative project, and record them in a list.

3. I use this list as an outline for generating the draft of my book. When beginning a chapter, I refer to my outline and make sure to include all three nonessential images. They are nonessential because the story could be told without them. Yet, and perhaps because of this challenge, generating material becomes more fun, as I have created a puzzle for myself as to how I am going to maintain order while including these distinct images. Maintaining linear organization is actually much simpler when I have something puzzling with which to concern myself. Perhaps I write a haiku for each nonessential image.

For example, from my outline for *Pants in a Tree*, I knew that at a given point in the story, I needed there to be a copper bathtub, an image of the full moon, and a smooth river stone. Having these images helped me supply the lighter touches of larger order that could provide a coherent reading experience without seeming overly plotted.

# THE HERO'S
# SPIRAL

I am a big fan of Joseph Campbell and his contributions to the study of storytelling. I admire how fully he lived, and how his full living enabled him to share so much with the world. He trusted his innate sense of direction, pursuing activities he was passionate about. He even coined the term "Follow your bliss."

Leading a life in which I pursue the things I love and let the rest fall away is not easy. At one point, years ago, Joseph Campbell was giving a talk, and someone in the audience criticized his use of the term "bliss," telling him that he was justifying narcissism. Campbell responded that he should have said, "Follow your blisters," because it amounted to the same.

Joseph Campbell identifies an archetype of storytelling that he calls the hero's journey. The outset of the hero's journey is the hero's call to adventure. This call is the voice of poetry. The call reverberates in the story through the actions of the hero.

In general, the hero's journey is an odyssey, ultimately bringing the hero back to the source. This journey is often elegantly represented as a circular path, though it should go in a spiral rather than a circle, because the world is different after the hero returns. A spiral shape indicates a geographic return, but energetically there is no going back. This distinction bears importance for understanding the work of emergence.

Days appear to be cyclical in that tomorrow the sun will rise, and I will know that I am experiencing morning "again." But tomorrow will not be the same morning anyone has ever had. I will never experience that precise morning ever again. Each reiteration spirals in and spirals out; I land on the familiar, yet I really am experiencing something original. The image is always there, anew.

# PLOTTING **EXERCISE**

The plot of a story is a causal sequence that results in change that engages the reader. It is beneficial for me personally to have a good amount of material already written before I set out to construct an outline: I get the clarity that comes from having an outline, and the sense of discovery from working from the heart of the story outward. All the while, I prioritize the breathing of words and images, the continually blooming form of the moment.

## PART ONE

Referring to the structure, name the significant moments of the work. I will want each plot point to carry roughly the same significance, and the arc of the book to rise and rise until, toward the end, it cannot rise any further, and the story resolves. I ask questions to generate ideas for how I can continually raise the stakes.

If I don't have one of the plot points yet, I ask: Is it right for the story as it wants to be told? If I seem to spend an inordinate amount of time on one or more plot points, I ask: What is right for the listener's engagement with the story's pace?

## PART TWO

After I have the important plot points (as few as three, five, or eight, and potentially more), I put together at least three subplots within each main point. I will also want to mine the material generated in previous marathons. (Even a single phrase could become a key subplot later in the book.) For example, I might have written about a ring. Is there a peculiar energy I associated with my description of the ring? Maybe it is important to the book.

When writing continually, I usually do not keep track of where I have been. The page is generous, and rereading brings surprises.

Any one given subplot might not be active within each main plot point (otherwise it might grow to compete with the main plot), but each subplot point will recur at least once in the book, so for each subplot point, be sure to find points when it can recur. For example, regarding the ring I wrote about, perhaps the ring's owner is later discovered. Perhaps the ring had been made from someone else's wedding band.

I am most interested in the subplot points, which is why I spend most of my time with them. Not all books are — or want to be — hero's tales, but my writing has certainly benefited from familiarity with the working of this archetype.

# STRUCTURE **EXERCISE**

Narratives hold the reader's attention in essentially two ways: through mystery and suspense.

- **mystery** encourages the listener to lean toward the **past** for resolution
- **suspense** invites the listener to anticipate the **future** for the dispersing of tension

I can utilize either or both. If I hit a snag during a marathon, I can turn to this exercise. I'll pull something from recent memory within the story's plot and use it as a structural device. For example, let's say I am writing during the marathon and, at this point, my two main characters (Alfonso and Beatrice) are sitting in their car...

- To create the structural tension of mystery, ask questions, but don't give the reader the information he needs to solve the mystery. For example, maybe Alfonso mistakes something about the car, and Beatrice is alarmed, because she is concerned that Alfonso has been stealing cars, or she wishes they had a better car, which raises money issues, and Beatrice thinks about her gambling addiction, convinced that the reason she has lost so much money is that the casino is against her...
- To create suspense, continually raise the stakes for the protagonist. Allow the protagonist some success, but then create more problems for her. For whatever reason, as readers, we want our protagonists to suffer. Using the above example, let's say that Alfonso is at a stoplight sending a text message, and the light has turned green, and Beatrice knows not only that he has no license, but also that there is a copious amount of cannabis in the trunk and that the grey car behind them seems to be ready to turn on its red and blue lights...

# WHEN PEOPLE BECOME FIGURES

I f viewed from a certain distance, any given person could be summed up by a figuration. It's an example of irony: I'm reading a story in which a character seems to be completely expressible within the already-understood description of a *type*. Reading, I understand that the character, as conveyed, is a real breathing individual, and yet, he's being conveyed as a type. Trimming off the individual aspects of a person can be funny, and, for sure, can impart some of the mystery of knowing someone.

How the characters are treated in a story raises the question of the narrator's relation to them. I learn something about the narrator when what I know of the characters revolves around one or two of their traits. Think of the characters in Woody Allen's films. His films feature one great (cutting) line after another. The way his characters squeeze themselves into figures sheds some light on actual human experience. Figuration is insightful shortsightedness.

If you've not seen his film *Midnight in Paris*, I won't be spoiling it for you to mention that several characters surrounding the protagonist serve as a constant antagonizing force. These characters repeatedly act in abstracted ways, which comes off as extreme — yet, they also accurately express how it feels to be in the main character's position. When it's right, figuration allows a greater contrast of energy and emotional force to play out.

Figuration is good when it encourages attentiveness to characters as they evolve. In general, character is that elusive thing most readers prize when reading a creative work. And character is what, as a writer, I seek to express by spending my time and energy producing work in my own way.

What distinguishes an authentic character has to do with how his/her details do not add up to anyone else's story. Instead, the authentic character, the individual, rises above externally imposed shaping. When an individual works to live what really amounts to someone else's life — or the life he imagines is supported by society — he's working to become a figure, which amounts to a removal from his personal energies the challenge of living true to intuition. An individual's identity is always beyond what can be characterized; at the same time, when I'm telling a story, I hope to try.

Suggestions are often made to writers that they should know everything about their characters. I should be able to list what my characters had for breakfast, describe their homes, and give a survey of the important occurrences in their pasts. Although some of this information is certainly useful — and is often helpful for conveying the eccentricities of real people — I would never suggest that these exercises are the right way to go about understanding someone. I could spend years learning about someone's belongings and would only have uncovered a greater mystery. (This idea is explored wonderfully in Robert Boswell's book *The Half-Known World*.)

It is possible to work both ways — to construct characters from figures (by letting them breathe in ways that do not fit with their service to the story), and to construct figures from characters (by summing them up: "She was the sort of woman who prided herself on how quietly she sipped her soup"). The right way depends largely on what you want the speaker's relationship to be with the story's world and with the characters within that world. Some stories want every character to be developed, and other stories want only figures. Usually, there is a mix of both, and the choice often has to do with how you want to pace your story, fast (cutting) or slow (dramatic).

- If the narrator is omniscient, knowing everything about the main players, what does the narrator do with that information? How does it affect the tone? How do I want it to affect the tone?
- If the narrator is not omniscient, what is being expressed by his/her relationship to the other characters (or figures) as conveyed to the reader?
- Is the reader felt to be a character (known intimately) or a figure (known, perhaps, as a projection)?
- Is there anything unknown that is necessary to conveying his/her humanity? Am I supplying characterizations in excess of what conveys a real human being?

# EXERCISE: PARALLEL OUTLINES

This exercise asks that you look solely at each character in your story, one right after another, to ensure that each one has an arc of expression honored in a way that fits with the chronology supplied by your story as a whole.

Where I have a scene of interaction between characters, and the story is about a past or future tension, I may need to reveal information in a peculiar order. If a key bit of information about a character happened in the past, but does not come into active play until two-thirds into the main story arc, I may wait until then to mention the bulk of it, for the sake of pacing and mystery.

1.  Begin with a secondary character. What is his/her story? What order works best, based on what you know about the overall story's superstructure?

2.  Develop a brief story path for each character. Where is she/he (as the protagonist in his/her own story)?

3.  Sketch out any changes that may have come about for the main character, based on your explorations of the secondary characters (or are they figures?).

4.  Does the narrator have an arc that changes as the story progresses? Does his/her distance to the characters change, and why? Does his/her distance to the reader change?

# EXERCISE: MONOLOGUE

Many writers care most about the story within the characters (rather than the characters within the story). This exercise is helpful when you hit a snag with plot or development, or whenever the story lacks the kind of charge you knows is possible. It gets the writer to develop more intimate knowledge of the story within a character.

Write from within that character's voice, on and on, until you resolve the block. Basically, sit down with that character and allow him to tell his version of what's going on. Choose a character in your story that hasn't been fully fleshed out by the narrator/speaker. Place that character in a scene and get her to talk about her experience within the story. What's her perception of the other characters? What's her ambition? What's on her mind in general?

Ideas for using this material:

- Use it as-is, interspersed at different points in the story
- Change the point of view and give that material to the narrator
- Follow the light shed by this monologue and develop the story in other areas so that it does more justice to the full spectrum of its characters

# ORDERING THE EXPERIENCE

I t's good to give a lot of thought to how the structure you're providing is ordering the reader's experience.

## 1. CHAPTERS

A chapter — understood to be a kind of formal segmentation of the reading experience — helps to sustain tension. Chapters also give the reader a stopping point that feels like a breather rather than being conclusive in any way. When a chapter has a title, that title names a frame for the next episode.

The main thing to keep in mind when choosing where to end a chapter and begin the next — so the book feels like a continuous read — is to conclude a chapter when conflict has been resolved but only when the stakes have also been raised.

In concluding a chapter in which some conflict has been resolved, you give readers a bit of white space, and thus offer them an opportunity to take a breather. In concluding a chapter where the stakes have been raised, you demonstrate to the reader that the book has in no way given up its ghost or showed its cards.

Without chapter breaks, a sustained reading experience of continually raised tension can feel exhausting. The reader doesn't have permission to stop. The chapter break is the book's way of saying, *you may rest here if you like.*

Immersive reading experiences such as novels never offer such a rest with the feeling of completion. The implicit agreement is that if the reader is involved in the book, she wants to stay, and so the chapter break comes as kind of a tease, signifying that the book is attentive to the reader's energy. Because a chapter is only a provisional completion, the next chapter will creatively offer the pattern of build-and-release, as will the next. Chapters reveal the habits of the book as a linear experience.

# 2. HEADERS AND THE IMPLIED OUTLINE

Headers are not chapters, necessarily. They allow a kind of meditation on a theme, which lends itself to an order that feels like a structured conversation or a series of lectures. With each new header/subheader, the reader knows that he is getting into a new theme, and that it's related to the main thesis, and has a parallel structure (meaning that each main header has the same significance or weight). Likewise, each subheader is a section with its own independent existence, which branches from the larger topic. The book may want the reader to see the shape of its structure.

# 3. OTHER OPTIONS

Creatively, a writer has many opportunities for giving order to a book. The use of white space is the most basic way. White space signifies the passing of time without issue, and simply gives the reader a visual break. Between audio tracks on a record of music, a few seconds of silence allow the listener to clear his/her head before entering into another musical experience. Reading can offer the same clearing through white space. Chapters give white space and also the scaffolding of their own device, whether titled, numbered, or both. Paragraphs give white space as well; how long or short to make one's paragraphs is worth considering. I've noticed in recent years that books tend to give more white space by having shorter paragraphs. The silence offered by the absence of text creates a kind of self-consciousness and an emphasis on what was just previously said.

Another tool for ordering work is to make a formal shift. A classic method for this is the *haibun*, a Japanese tradition related to the haiku, which in its most basic form is a variance between prose and verse. Creatively, I can do the same thing by including images, quotes, shapes, boxes around text, highlighting excerpts, and things of that nature. This visual organization can be rewarding for the reader because of the variety it offers.

Your writing can also be a performance or an art piece (like an artist's book). As the writer, you can dictate the rules of engagement for your text. If you want it to be something participatory, you need to make the rules clear to the reader.

- Does my writing flow like a conversation? A novel? Does it follow the chronology of a person's life? Is the story's time parallel to the flow of time, or are there multiple threads of chronology? Does my piece want to be organic, meditational, flowing with a kind of outline supplied by headers and subheaders? Is my writing more a work of poetry? Am I including other media besides text? Is it a collage?

- How will I order the reader's experience? Do I draw on any other specific writers for formal inspiration?

# A FEW DEFINITIONS

*Approach* — The way in which I set out to write something. For example, when following a prose poem approach, I prioritize images and resonance above wording, using language in which the imagination or dreaming dictates.

*Emergence* — What arises from the writer's chemistry with the listener. Language can be seen as a form of emergence from symbols and sounds and patterns in chemical impulses. Chemistry can be seen as an emergence of physics — the play of elements. One emergence is not necessarily more complex than another, because what we see depends on the mode of our consciousness. If a formula for emergence exists, it is to trust openly and to invite wildness so that there is interaction among the modes of consciousness.

*Method* — An overarching technique. The writing marathon is an example of method.

*Mode* — The way that I write based on my expectations of form and function. The structure that the work takes is not necessarily predetermined by my mode of writing.

*Piece* — A bit that stands on its own is a piece. Whether long or short, it's simply referred to as a piece. The writer's life is a piece. A day is a piece. A glimpse is a piece. The internal dialogue of a public speaker is a piece of the reality amid another piece, a simultaneous one, that the speaker is giving a public speech. Private and public are pieces against each other, and sometimes they are pieces with each other, and become of a piece. Musically, the two pieces can be perceived as a musical chord or at least an interval in music — two or more notes sounding together. The frequencies and timbres resonate within and against each other, and what is produced can be felt as a piece in itself — a piece of a larger ensemble, of a larger work — a life's work, and the work of oneness. Depending on one's perspective, all is at work or pieces are at work.

*Shape* — The reader's perception of the written piece's structure. Some moments will appear larger or more significant to different readers, and so a work of the same structure will have different shapes.

*Structure* — How the writer organizes the elements of the written piece. Musical structure deals with the flow of images. Supportive structure handles and manages interactions.

# 4. IT'S MADE TO IGNITE

# IGNITION

⬛ *In poetry, non-knowing is a primal condition; if there exists a skill in the writing of poetry, it is in the minor task of associating images.*

— GASTON BACHELARD

know something of the challenge of putting together images that associate with each other and relate to the listener. But in the middle of the experience, in the cloud of immersion, image-association happens spontaneously, and is certainly a minor task compared to abiding productively in nonknowing, whatever the form.

The literary poem-in-a-book is one thing. There is poetry in the choice and preparation of food. Rock music is another poetic iteration. Each moment in which the rhythm upturns or funks a militant up-and-down pattern is a kind of poetic opening. The story of economy and of things adding up is ruined a bit in these moments, because the significant image exudes life; in a way, the story ignites — through the tension of language and the friction of peculiar resonances.

*A man walks down the street.*

The poetic image might be taken as it is, literally, or it could be received as an image or symbol. Perhaps we see this image as a metaphor of life as well. It resonates with us in that way. And, in a small way, we wonder who the man is, where he came from, where he's going, whether what he carries with him is helping him along.

We can also look at the shape of the thought and think of it poetically in that way. As a shaped thought, it's pretty straight-forward; plainly spoken. It's functioning in language in as about a fundamental way as it can. This language is also going some-where — it does not expect us to slow down and examine the way that the phrase has been laid out.

*Going, going, going, the man on the street.*

The phrase begins with action — action absent a subject. It takes itself as the subject for the time-being, and we suspend compre-hension of all else. The action of *going* is mixed with the word's repetition, and when we at last come to the man on the street, his figure is mixed in — it's his whirlwind of action.

*That man and his walk!*

Here we sense the individuation of the man against other poten-tial men potentially walking. The speaker is remarking about a particular man, and in the remark we get a sense of the speaker's individuation as well. We wonder who this person is that he or she reacts in such a way to the walking man.

I'm not really changing the information so much as playing with the free space offered by language. It's there; we don't often see how much wiggle room there truly is, because most of the time we seek to convey meaning with the shapes of our thoughts. We are simply getting from point A to point Z.

*Once, there was a man who walked down the street.*

I love the way this phrasing signifies the beginning of a tale.

From thin air, a claim is conjured: Once, such-and-such happened. Once, so-and-so existed. There's something about the removal of the word *Once* that makes its claim so different than, for example, simply mentioning it: A man walked down the street. The words invite the reader to imagine a parallel space, perhaps in the past — and certainly again in this moment of retelling.

*The street had a man walking down it.*

Here, the focus is on the street. The man is really just a passing thing, and what's significant is the street, or perhaps the fact that a man was walking on it. Maybe it is a dead-end street, or a street where only women walk.

*A man walks uphill down the street.*

This sentence shows something peculiar in the telling. It draws our attention to the man and his actions, but primarily we're hung up on why it was phrased that way. This kind of play had better pay off for the reader, because it takes work that distracts us from the feeling that we're going somewhere.

*It was a man that walked down the street.*

This could be a factual interpretation of the street scene. Just prior to this statement, something must have happened that called into question the gender or manliness of the figure on the street. I'm inclined to read into this phrase beyond the literal distinction from man/not-man and ascribe to the man a kind of Dirty Harry swagger.

Compare it to a similarly constructed sentence:

*It was a street that the man was walking on.*

Here the speaker is creating the possibility that men can walk on many things: airplane wings, chairs, blades of grass.

*Well, a man is walking down the street, after all.*

Here we get an image of the world in which the street and the man live. The speaker seems reluctant or dubious about someone walking down the street. Was it too dark? Dangerous? Is the speaker concerned that he/she is alone? Was a house robbed? Why is the speaker seemingly relieved to notice something so commonplace?

*It's just a man walking down the street.*

Here's a phrase we too often imply internally when we're searching for ideas. We're saying that it's nothing more. As a statement, of course, it's fine, it serves a purpose, it keeps our attention earthbound.

Let's see what happens when drawing attention to this language. A good way to draw more attention to something as writers is to spend more time with it in writing, consciously returning to the insistent word "just" whenever possible:

*It's just a man walking down the street. He's just walking. He's doing what you'd expect, and not doing anything besides going down the street. He's just a normal man. It's just a normal street. People walk on streets. This man is doing just that.*

When I write resolutely this way, as a writer, I'm inclined to see the insistence as a kind of pressure cooker. I'm inclined to say what is *not* happening:

*It's not like he's stolen your wallet. He's just walking like anyone else would walk. He's not a stuffed dummy; he's walking down the street. Go ahead and look if you don't believe me. See, it's just a man — it's not a whole parade of people even though you keep saying it sounds like that.*

There are many potential avenues to explore. I risk expressing that I'm uncertain — and that doubt makes me uncomfortable. The more I learn that it's OK to play with ideas, the more at ease I become with being uncertain. It's about prioritizing the shape of thoughts over the words that are used to form them. As a performance, this writing may take a bit of time to arrive at the crystalline shape that does justice to my interaction.

# IMAGE AND TIME

**S**ound travels at a speed. Light travels at a speed. Light is fast, but it has to reach from point P to point Q, and it takes time to get there. I think of light as instantaneous, though I also know that it's not instantaneous.

An image, as far as we are concerned, is an imaginative rendering. An image is also an artifact, something that has been made. It is also something that is observed, both by the writer and by the reader. A synonym for image is metaphor.

I prioritize the sense faculty of vision when referring to imagery. It is often assumed that an image is a visual image, though whether an image is seen or felt or tasted is not the whole story. So what is the story of an image? This story is what language performs.

More than in words, we work in images; or, rather, we work through words to shape images. A musical idea hits me and gives rise to a song, and the song performs that thought's shape. It did not take science to discover that fingers in a given position on the fretboard were the logical cause of beauty. I have to follow the shape of the image as it wants to be performed through time.

Of its own accord, language just is what it is. This is a different understanding than the insistence that language means something. Language is a kind of attentiveness, a mode of attention. All art is, at least at the first moment, a way of paying attention. It comes across in syntax: There are a number of ways of phrasing something, of being attentive to it musically. Different words come to me, depending on the rhythm of my work, and the presence of the given words helps to structure the order of phrases. These choices ripple forth.

I have to do something with my attention. I am alive, and that's a good thing — and I write. Art affirms the will to live. Beauty inspires me to give presence. And when I'm exposed to words, the linguistic landscape becomes thought.

People say words are no substitute for the real thing. Maybe they're right. But while I'm reading or writing, words are the real thing; I'm in a digital or read-write mode, where my senses are textual. Language engages and speaks to me. In life and in writing, I encounter metaphors that shape my experience.

# AVOIDING CANNED AVOCADO

I have heard words likened to canned avocado. Comparing the direct experience of the Grand Canyon to my telling you about it is like offering you canned avocado rather than one that is ripe and fresh.

In turn, direct experience of something fails to deliver on claims-in-writing. Maybe I had in mind the idealized image of life as a scuba instructor, and I worked to achieve that goal, but when I got to it, I found that life to be hollow compared with my imagining of it.

So it helps to be open minded. Perhaps we can distinguish a kind of writing that walks the talk. And that writing would have to be original — to avoid canned avocado I can't can it. Criteria #1 is that it be fresh, an approach rather than a form. Arriving at the original means I've got to let go of what I'm holding.

Tom Waits said on a Fresh Air interview that sometimes he'd take a tape recorder and put it in a trash can on rolling wheels, go outside by himself, and roll it around — then listen to the tape to hear what kind of rhythms had been uncovered. It doesn't hurt to be patient.

1. Meaning is supplied by people
2. In life and writing, search for significant images by forming patterns in the accrued structure of the after-image
3. The life liberated from prescribed meaning is open to the fresh moment's mystery

I'm outside, and I see a tiny blossom of yellow clover. A honeybee is making a stop at the flower — then on to the next nectar-station. I watch the bee, admiring its colors, how it's yellow is a kind of honey color in itself. I look up at the sunrise, and there's an ounce of that color mixed into the brilliant swath of hues from the sunshine making its way to earth, its light bouncing off the hills and concentrating somewhat more thoroughly in the humidity. Two distant fir trees remind me of the fur on the honeybee legs. None of these images necessarily add up. But performing alongside the rhythm of our thoughts and interactions, these images add to the way we naturally move from one thought to another.

So I see something of a bee in all that comes after. The shape of its image gets abstracted in my interactions with the world — with my relationships and observations. And the way I saw the bee in the first place had to do with all I had seen in the past — the component parts were constructed of abstractions that were familiar to me — and those yet to occur to me, yet are there in my field of nature. What I see is always original and always a cocreation, and it's shaped by reverberation with the after-images of what I've seen.

Say there's a white screen door. I don't want to presume I already know what that is, or I will miss the opportunity to resonate with that image and be closed to whether it's at the front of a house in a small town with as much road noise as a busy city or resting on the side of the road in a moving van waiting for the driver to get off the phone to continue on its way to Virginia, where it will be painted blue.

On the other hand, I don't want to be so dialed in that I'm not going anywhere, and I miss all the points but my own. It's good to remember that these images are resonating — and are never static. One thing becomes another thing as the time goes on — the door swings and, in its reflection, I catch sight of my loved one coming home. Landing on an image, I keep listening to it, letting it resonate. I learn about it, about myself, about the world, and I change who I am from this interaction. The world is never the same. Hearing, I also feel.

I construct by using the forms I have available. Being resonates with and against all things, creating harmony or dissonance. I take comfort that even dissonance leads to a greater, more ambitious achievement of harmony. The journey through dissonance into greater harmony is the hero's journey.

The journey puts me at odds with the world, even if my life is relatively tame. Imagine a mode where I no longer measure my days through a contribution to the economy and, instead, am moved by love. I follow the hero's path, and I may fail in the worldly sense. If a trace of the ego remains, *this* hero remains the obstacle for a greater hero.

A long time ago, the earth was parched because a dragon was blocking the flow of the rivers. Indra came along, slew the dragon, and realized his position as king of the gods. He hired a builder to construct a palace worthy of his good deed. Well, the builder was immortal, and Indra was immortal, so the building went on and on, becoming increasingly elaborate in an infinite attempt to illustrate the king's importance. Indra didn't want it all to stop — because, after all, how much was really enough?

The builder wasn't entirely sure that it was correct for him to give of himself endlessly for this single pursuit, so he looked to Brahma, the impersonal and universal creator. Brahma took form and stepped in, showing Indra what the infinite-of-infinites truly meant — and freed Indra from the need to prove his position.

> And if we seem a small factor in a huge pattern, nevertheless it is of relative importance. We take a tiny colony of soft corals from a rock in a little water world. And that isn't terribly important to the tide pool. Fifty miles away the Japanese shrimp boats are dredging with overlapping scoops, bringing up tons of shrimps, rapidly destroying the species so that it may never come back, and with the species destroying the ecological balance of the whole region. That isn't very important in the world. And thousands of miles away the great bombs are falling and the stars are not moved thereby. None of it is important or all of it is.
>
> — JOHN STEINBECK

# EXERCISE: YOUR STORY'S IMAGINATIVE LANDSCAPE

> *The debt we owe to the play of imagination is incalculable.*

— CARL JUNG

When experiencing a story, we enter a kind of trance or immersion, an altered state of consciousness. In many cases, we forget that we are physically reading words, actually hearing language spoken, and we sense, transparently at times, that we are within the story's landscape as created by the language, as invoked by the speaker.

Consider the following questions:

- What is known about the landscape in your imaginative creation?
- What is still unknown?
- What does the reader sense about your landscape, and how is it different from the waking world?

# SENSORY
# LANDSCAPE

> ◢ *While I was lying there in a bison robe, a coyote began to howl not far off,*
> *and suddenly I knew it was saying something. It was not making words, but it*
> *said something plainer than words.*
>
> — BLACK ELK

seem to forget that what I make with words depends on my being a bodied creature. But when witnessing a powerful story, my body reacts. When I am performing basic sums, I notice very little physiological response. Establishing more cognitive wiggle room with regard to how I interpret and perceive is useful. It's not about performing static stretches. It's about the interaction between my mind and body as two forms of the same thing. Getting mind and body to move as one is very powerful. I re-emerge into a higher natural state.

Ideally, my internal witness must be as strong as the sensory phenomena I experience. The only way to actually achieve that equivalence is to challenge the witness to stretch his ability, such as in a writing marathon. I hold a train of thought not from sheer willpower or narrowness of focus, but as part of being open to all experience without kudos-ing myself or rejecting the balloon of sensation. It gets harder, and the train of thought should only be held for as long as the witness is present. When I let go, I open myself even more to receive another refreshing flow of sensation.

Emotions and stories are stored in the senses. When encountering them, I need to bring the conscious mind into play as a witness so that I can stretch through them, freeing the sensations, recognizing imagistic elements working beyond stories.

It's natural to experience freedom of mind and body. Yet, there are disturbances in the field of perception, both cognitive and sensory. I witness conflicting beliefs. I experience physical discomfort in life. So I shut down, perhaps to be protected against future trauma or an understanding that would conflict with a past belief. This closure creates a different kind of suffering unless I work to free myself by bringing the witness back into and beyond these tight places where energy is spent and held.

I have to guess at the shape of my latent energy until I come to know more about it through the resonances I feel as I interact and relate with the world. The central ability is to use my conscious awareness to become aware of the unknown movers. There may always be stones left unturned in my psyche, simply because it is rather difficult to go to the prelinguistic body, the sense elements, and to know what's what.

This is a spiritual pursuit because of the nature of directing attention upward and into the mysterious, remaining uncertain. The goal is to become a better, more ethical, healthy, fulfilled person, with the kind of happiness that does not require anyone or anything —including my own self-concepts.

Fulfillment is not an eventual goal. It happens whenever I apply myself wholeheartedly to what I believe in — beyond my fears, releasing my hold on anything familiar or comforting. In the experience of true freedom, perfect responsibility emerges, where all that is moving is my natural self. I am being lived and moved by my deepest truth. And experience will remind me that it will have the final say. This is yoga practice.

It is said that everyone who sincerely practices yoga will eventually have to ask the same questions that Arjuna asked Krishna in the *Bhagavad Gita*. The *Bhagavad Gita* uses the metaphor of a battle to teach the internal path that became Tantra Hatha yoga. The scene of the *Bhagavad Gita* is a battle, but this story is not about an actual battle. You would never be able to convince someone to fight in a war advocating complete nonattachment. The lessons in the text lay the groundwork for practice in which the body is the field.

Things arise in the practice of writing that challenge my conception of my place in the world. I naturally want to live in a way that supports and strengthens the quality of my inner life. It can be perplexing to understand the world, but that's not my primary task. At least while I am writing, I set aside all worldly issues and go completely inside. I affirm that my intentions are good. The truth of my experience will naturally spill over into the world. I do not need to steer the result — all I need to do is steer myself so that I give all my energy to the practice.

Becoming familiar with the concept that there is a source for truth, I lean my attention toward the source rather than the truth — as something beyond the truth. Can I express the same truth in another way? Another way? And another? What changes when I rephrase the truth, and what remains the same?

As I stretch myself to write, I hold onto my sense of truth, but I don't hold so that a fuller expression can't make itself known. When I've found a more real expression of truth, I regard it highly, but I let it go where it pleases.

# STEWARDS OF ENERGY

> *I used to work very hard thinking and planning. Now ideas come when I least expect them. If I need to know something, I ask. As soon as I ask an answer comes. If it does not come it is not for me at this time. It is as if a life giver were speaking to me. This makes my work and life very easy.*
>
> — OMORI-SAN

When something is puzzling or concerning, I'll sit down and obsess over it, expecting an answer. The puzzle tends to just run in circles, because as much as it is a real concern, it is also an energy phenomenon within me. My energy has everything to do with how I relate to the thing. *The Hobbit* has a scene in which Bilbo is lost in a forest, and he climbs a tree to see if he can find the edge of the forest from that perspective. He can't — but the reason he can't see the border of the forest is that he's in a valley.

The solution to a complex problem will surface at an unexpected moment. Maybe I come home from work one day, and the light bulb burns out as I enter the house. From the circumstance, I get a deep and true glimpse of my life. At that precise moment, as I am standing alone in the dark, everything changes. I give up my current career, something I've worked decades trying to perfect, not because it has to do with light bulbs, but because I have carried the intent with me in the back of my head. In energetic terms, it's just floating around in me as something I'm hanging onto. The moment of realization is a moment of cleared energy, a new perspective.

I should also remember that what holds me back is the limiting belief that the fruit of the practice should be what I enjoy. Instead, I wholeheartedly offer the work itself and give it openly, welcoming whatever it causes me to experience, and allowing those sensations to flow through me, witnessed, without causing me to act based on preference.

Viewing myself as the steward of my energy (rather than the rightful permanent owner of my body) naturally gets me to let go of what isn't right for me at an energetic level. I want my energy to be high and balanced while I'm at work. I want energy to be low when I rest, but within this low energy, the deathless integrity of the internal witness must remain.

# NOT THE MASTER
# OF ENERGY

> ◢ As long as the moving Prana having entered the middle path does not become steady in the cavity of god, the Bindu will not be steady under the firm restraint of the Prana and the Chitta also will not be concentrated in natural meditation. Until then any knowledge about Yoga is like boastful and incoherent talk.
>
> — HATHA YOGA PRADIPIKA, *Verse 114*

It happens that I can get a pretty inflated ego when working toward my practice. I feel that *I* am on the right path, and that this success glorifies me. Pretty soon, this kind of attitude disintegrates a practice. Just because I can pretend that I know what I'm doing doesn't mean that I have any control over anything.

The same force that sustains my life will one day allow me to die. Practice moves me to experience and enact freedom while I am still in the body. Life is a gift, and life continues to be a gift. Acting accordingly, I set aside my false belief that I'm owed anything, and I can move transparently within the giving, in turn giving by my own nature. A musician plays the accordion, and the world may respond as the ego dreams that the world should respond.

I might be able to make a living with my passion, but in all cases, there will be things about that way of making a living that I don't enjoy, yet are nonetheless required. So whether I'm a tax accountant, an author, or a yoga teacher, I can find some peace knowing that my effort will never be entirely pain-free. Driving that point home as a reality can help calibrate my expectations. The best financial advice is to be free from the concern for money. Feeling this way has huge consequences for how I live and what I do with my time, because it means that, energetically, I'm open.

I don't have the final say. But I can live fully for now, and understand what it might mean to let the spirit move me, and the universe to express itself through me. Liberated or not, I'm still here, and I still have certain characteristics. A liberated father is a better father. A more realized mother and writer is a complete gift to everyone around her.

It's never so clear when we should pretend to know who and what we really are. Innovation meets people where they're coming from. In some cases, the right thing for the advanced yogi to do is start a lavender farm or soap distribution company or a nonprofit organization geared to the preservation of rain-forest land in perpetuity. Having been freed and/or achieved any kind of success, I find that the first question to ask myself is whether I'm doing anything to help others. When I look back, I see everyone who helped me along the way.

I went to an acupuncturist to receive treatment for what seemed to be an issue involving the spleen, at least so in Chinese medicine, and both times during the treatment I had the same revelation. I was on the table with a few needles, relaxing, letting the nerves, stimulated, do their thing. It's difficult to describe exactly how it happened, but somehow because of the relaxation I cozied into a place where something — a statement — surfaced and became at once obvious and precious: a revelation.

It surfaced. That is how I describe it — like it was already there, but for one reason or another, wasn't immediately present. It is likely that this surfacing represents something we all know or perhaps sense when our energy — and therefore our thoughts — are balanced in a healthy flow. When the acupuncture clarified my energy, the thought surfaced in the form of a statement. The statement, in turn, produced a physiological affirmation of the energy-work, which led to the statement being produced or revealed. Therefore, the act of giving or articulating one's connection to a transpersonal truth is innately blissful insofar as it stimulates a person's actions with its energetic trigger.

The self disappeared — and it became something I took for granted — mere elements. It became obvious just how often I was turning away from the real object of life work to make sure I was still here, and sort of fussing around with one thing or another. The possibilities for self-concern never have to go away, but I don't have to be attentive to them, because that attention comes at the expense of deeper living. I naturally have a disposition, qualities, skills, a style. These aspects manifest whether I like it or not. Self-work and introspection can develop these things and even make me into something else — sometimes more in line with my will and sometimes just different. But once I've learned the fundamentals of my life's work — as a writer, say — I can move forward.

I can arrive at a place where life is lived in service — without excessive self-regard, loving myself as I am, and more interested in what I can do than what I might be able to act from. In the end, the self dissolves in complete and continual appreciation of life. What one does with that appreciation will happen automatically, because it must, as an open-ended expression, or an offering. It happens through me, from life to all that happens after, and before, and throughout. I get to be the witness, and that is no small thing.

In scenes in the *Mahabharata* leading up to the battle of the *Bhagavad Gita*, both Arjuna and Duryodhana go to Krishna to ask for his help. These two were fighting each other and are now appealing to the same person. Krishna offers one of them his vast and impressive army and the other one himself as an advisor. Duryodhana chooses the army, and Arjuna chooses Krishna as his advisor. The abilities of the advisor, or the internal nonacting witness, are superior, regardless of the numbers.

Arjuna was a kshatrya, a member of the warrior caste. He lived to fight. His bravery in battle was second to none. For twelve years prior to the battle of the Kurukshetra, his mind was fixed on only one thing: defeating his opponents. He practiced extreme austerities. He stood on the top of a mountain in tree posture for twelve years. According to myth, such *tapas* bestow great powers on a yogi. Yet, when Krishna shows him the field of battle, when everything is about to begin, Arjuna becomes terrified — not by the size of the army, but because he sees friends and family out there. He doesn't want to have to leave behind everything. He is terrified of who he would become when the battle is over.

When I write in earnest, I put myself in Arjuna's position, and embrace nothing but the uncertainty, the openness. I cannot be entirely certain that who I become after practice is the same person as before. If it enters a body, a psyche also enters the body's conditioning, along with its dispositions, thoughts, and memories. It seems that I may be the same person. Each moment opens into the eternal.

Before the battle, Arjuna prays, until at last one day he finishes praying and, having fasted for years, goes out hunting and shoots a pig with his bow. The pig is his catch — except that another hunter has shot the pig at the exact same time from the other side. The pig has been shot through the heart simultaneously by two arrows. Arjuna is very hungry and argues with the other hunter, who is just as belligerent as Arjuna. The argument quickly turns into a fight. Arjuna goes at the hunter with every weapon he has, but no sooner does he use a weapon than it is taken or broken by his opponent. Arjuna at last strikes the hunter with his sword, but it, too, is destroyed. In shame and frustration, Arjuna at last brings out a small shrine to Siva and, as an offering, adorns it with flowers, only to find that the flowers have not landed on his statue but on the hunter — his opponent. Arjuna realizes that his opponent is none other than Siva himself and throws himself at his feet. Siva is pleased and rewards Arjuna with a magical weapon.

Siva is the god of yoga practice. When writing, I remember that I may be up against something that can never be defeated. Instead, I know that the further I progress, the more devotion I will feel. We deserve to be happy. To live in a way that makes me deeply fulfilled takes work, often a great deal of work, because I have to be in lock-step with what is required of me.

Doing this work is a kind of sacrifice. Something is calling me to do this work. It's myself, but not my everyday self. Poetry calls me to do work that leads to deep fulfillment. Distinguishing between the two is important. The voice guiding me toward genuine self-improvement, the voice that challenges me toward truth, is who I really am.

Forces within me urge me toward and away from things. Is that really me wanting, or is it just urge itself? Urges are conditional. The body wants to breathe. My cells know this. I exhale, and feel the growing urge to inhale. I inhale, and feel the growing urge to exhale. I crave foods and activities, but what I'm really craving are states of being. The appreciation of other people can feel very nice, but I want to pick and choose what other people like about me. And this feeling, too, changes.

Total freedom is where I keep myself open and do what's actually in my best interest. I am simply in a place where I will do what must be done, forgoing the rest. In the between times, I am patient and forgiving with myself.

The ego wants to pick and choose stories, phrases, and events to support our self-concept. We shy away from the things that threaten us, and we gravitate toward the things that bolster our sense of self. Departure from these two extremes is uncomfortable territory, yet it leads to personal growth, because it means overcoming the limitations placed on who we think we are, making room for who we essentially are.

For the sake of balance, we should rely on others and on social norms. Otherwise, things get weird and potentially do more harm than good. A little bit of freedom can be mishandled in a big way when I believe that my right to be completely free on the inside has much to do with the rest of the world. It is an introspective practice, and so I leave behind everything in society when I'm at work. But returning, I can't forget to pick it back up so that I can — it is hoped — serve the greater good. One truly happy person is a priceless gift.

In the ancient days, when poets lived in huts in the mountains, life was very different. The way we live now, we trust modern medicine, nutrition, and an efficient postindustrial infrastructure. We have high expectations for a life lived in relative comfort, if not luxury. The practice of poetry is still relevant; it helps address quality of life issues by dealing directly with the mindful body.

We owe it to ourselves to take full advantage of the relative ease and comfort we have available to go deep in our practice. Without necessarily renouncing the world and living in a cave, we can devote a substantial portion of our lives to writing practice. Also, we can integrate that concentrated, focused time into our daily lives, hopefully with a good handle on our ego urges.

With life itself there is a strong urgency to do the impossible, which is to live forever in this body. If death presents us with a monumental challenge, even just facing the idea of it, and if death itself will be a great challenge, why not do everything we can — now — to overcome its limitations on how fully we live?

What's wonderful about practice is that I don't need to die to benefit from the lessons given by death. I can face my reflection of death; I can overcome it each day, so that whenever my time is up, I will greet it as inevitable, not as something to be avoided.

I ask myself: Do I enjoy life as much as I could if I transcended the aversion to death and lived with complete detachment and total freedom? And I seek deathless truth.

# EXERCISE: DOUBLE YOU

You suddenly find that you are forming into twins. From this moment on, there's no more "you." Now there are two identical people. They're standing at a fork in the road waving goodbye. One chooses to devote his/herself entirely to the deepest internal practice possible at any given moment, spending as much time and energy as he/she can in deeper and deeper states of practice. The other chooses to devote his/herself as much as possible to succeeding in the world: being regarded highly by other people, amassing a wealth of money, experience, and outward achievement.

Give these two people a substantial amount of time to pursue their paths with all the resources they have available to them. Suppose that the two meet up again after a decade or two. Side by side, inside and out, how do they compare?

# THE ORGANS FOR ACTION

According to Sankya practice, we have five "organs for action," meaning we have essentially five options for things to do:

- Procreation, including everything related, such as dating, kissing, etc.
- Elimination, which of course includes pooping and peeing, also sweating and other excretions
- Locomotion, entailing all movement
- Grasping, entailing manipulation, change of location or structure
- Speech, which includes mumbling, moaning, yelling, and all communication

Living according to Sankya, you don't get trapped in the affliction of a compelling story, of desire, of any sort of clinging or loss. I can eat and digest an apple. I can speak. This, as a story, could become very complicated.

My practice deepens by discriminating actions, meanings, and scenes into component parts. Just understanding that it is possible to make such distinctions is powerfully liberating. Whenever I feel trapped, unsatisfied, or confused, I can return to the five organs for action and witness the natural play of pure being.

# THE SWITCHING STATION

I was relaxed and in a good mood. I leaned back and put some of my weight onto my hand. My hand learned something — it had been placed against a hot stove. Reflex retracted the hand. Before I could assess the imprudence, a basic part of my mind reacted.

The mind receives sense information and sends signals to the senses, creating a response. It is what makes the body work as a sensing, locomoting machine. Whether you are being helpful or harmful, the mind performs its function.

Deepening my practice, I naturally withdraw my perspective to where it is distinct from the sensing, feeling, moving sense of self. Different, and yet the same, this witness gives potentiality to the self's expressions. The extent to which I move as that witness has to do with how much I step back my perspective. Withdrawing my perspective into the knower, I also withdraw my ability to claim a sense of self at all — even alive only for this moment, alive for an eternity.

I inevitably return to the truth that I am on a path already. As much as possible, I strive to pursue love's deepest expression to such an extent that there is nothing left over, no sense of self. No worries about who I am. All that I do and think are offerings, expressions of the divine paid back to the divine. I give to my heart's fullest extent.

The mind works with words, it facilitates the language of sensation and does so to support one's sense of self. The mind is always relaying information from the senses and self-organizing this information. This response is neither good nor bad; actually, it can be both. When a bus speeds down the street, and a person is in the middle of that street, it is good for that person that the mind can be the switching station to protect the person's cohesive ego in such a way that guides him to safety. If that person who just narrowly escaped the bus happened to be Adolf Hitler, we might have a different opinion of whether the mind, in this case, was a good or a bad thing.

Becoming more mindful is liberating because it helps us to become more balanced. We are integrating the mind's functionality with the self's true desire for liberation. Along with self-restraint and contemplativeness is lovingkindness. Balanced energy, transcendence — these things are intrinsically good. And there is something better: to identify oneself as wholly dissolved, one with impersonal nature, with intrinsic awareness only circumstantially situated within a person.

The ego's job is to get you out of the way of that bus, to praise you for doing so, and to surround you with people and an environment that supports your sense of self. In practice, you enter a place protected from the ego-threats of the world, a place designed to develop the internal witness. It is good to have a practice that is separate from the world, where you can give your full attention to what's real, devoid of worldly context. It is hard to maintain this attention either in practice or in the world, but it is at least significantly more straightforward in your practice.

Because the world supplies many convincing stories, fully integrating the privacy of practice with worldly interaction is hard. Thus sacred space is important. At its root, sacred means *set apart* or *separate*. A space is made sacred by giving it some boundaries from the world.

The hero of any story has to enter the dark woods before he or she is able to claim the hidden fruit. You want your sacred space to challenge you. Its sense of support guides you into greater dissolving and deeper communion. Its protection allows you to devote 100% of your focus and energy to what's happening on the inside, so you can cultivate a strong ability to embrace the bliss of dissolving and union. In that way, you can re-emerge into the world as one whose center of gravity is beyond the edge of your expertise, where fear has no effect because the object of fear has been burned off.

Miraculously, by virtue of the practice itself, you create an ego that is secure enough in what's higher that it will not look for stories in the world to validate the ego. When the sense of self is more accustomed to being dissolved in practice and is never far from this deepening relationship, the world will gradually lose the ability to threaten the ego. There just won't be anything there anymore.

Fragments and charges from ego issues will remain in the self for a long time. In being threatened, your ego may discover a story that it finds suitable as a means of defense. You may believe that you've gone far enough, perhaps farther than most, and that's good enough. At any rate, no one can really prove you right or wrong. If you're really seeking liberation, you're only going to trust that very thing that threatens to overwhelm the ego with bliss and lovingkindness — the menace of fully awakened energy.

When the ego trusts what is beyond and above the ego, the force that is acting is not the ego.

# EXERCISE: CHECKING OUT

It is good to retreat into practice when you do so to develop a closer relationship to your life purpose, and when remaining in the world would not accomplish this aim.

- Born of the world, who retreats from the world?
- Retreating from the world, what do you retreat to?
- What do you bring with you when retreating from the world?
- How have you changed in re-emerging into the world? How are you the same?

What work remains to be done today, knowing that death will eventually occur? This action is your yoga of devotion when you perform the acts out of responsibility opened beyond expectation.

Recognizing that your life, with its comforts and pains, is impermanent, let this knowledge be at work in your practice. What is this eternal source of your soul's most trusted bliss?

Recognizing that transcendence is your heart's desire, you must give your writing practice your total focus. Leave aside ambitions and future-thinking. Let fullness of transient experience be your only goal.

Even a little of this practice will change your life in a positive way. You may arrive at a place where you realize that nothing needs to be done. Because using words comes naturally for me (whether I think of myself as eloquent or not, words extend from the totality of nature), my use of language becomes yoga.

Each time you write, it happens in a way that has never been so before in all of history — and will never happen again just the same way. This instant of experience is precious.

Recognize in the experience that you are grateful that you get to do it. Allowed to practice, understanding what you do, be open to what can reveal itself to you today. Choose amid the freedom of feelings to be flooded with devotion.

Afterward, in your daily life, carry the memory of this devotion as an energy that flows through your cells. Encouraging your cells to remember the flood of devotion, you will accomplish the impossible.

# WHAT IS WORTH KNOWING

I am faced with undeniable opportunities to learn things. If I chose, I could spend the rest of my life learning one thing or another. However, I can't say how much longer I'll be alive and therefore able to learn, and there's no promise that I'll be able to learn everything. So, with limited time, what is most important? It might be the kind of learning that comes from doing.

When I see someone deep into his/her practice, I see the power and joy of a soul stripped bare. In practice, we're given the choice: Should we step outside of the familiar, over which we have some level of comfort and mastery, into true knowledge?

The Zen monk Eihei Dogen was a true master. As a teacher, he regarded his teachings as barriers to the truth.

> *Set words and phrases are not the way of understanding. There is something free from all of these things.*
>
> — DOGEN

It is good to know things. It is good, too, to work toward residing fully alive in a place of nonknowing opened by practice. Sanskrit is an excellent language for understanding abstract concepts. I recently discovered this Sanskrit word:

*a*

This is the first and last word. It refers to the sound of breath. It is an open, unconstricted vowel; the root of all speech.

One concern of science is to understand the constituent particles of matter; the atom is not the smallest particle, the proton is not the smallest, the quark, and so on... Looking in the opposite direction, we can find more questions about infinity, or finity. We interact with a very real world of forms, whether or not we can reduce matter to fundamental parts.

Seeing the world in this way can be useful for providing wiggle room away from the stories and meanings we construct. For example, I may notice that my hamstrings have become tight. The sensations from the gently stretched hamstrings aren't something I need to be attached to or form meaning from. This sensation is the feeling of stretching hamstrings. I watch the feeling and let it flow through me, unaltered, making adjustments to honor the truth of the posture. Freed awhile from story, cells experience the wisdom above both consciousness and unconsciousness.

True relaxation is not merely relaxation. It is the knower impartially witnessing the flow of energy within relaxation. Relaxing the ego, I make room for higher nature to move my mind and my limbs.

# 5. NONACTION WITHIN ACTION

# NONACTION WITHIN ACTION FOR ARTISTS

Look at the way a child will use her imagination and pretend that she is a wizard or a dolphin. For a child, no real separation exists between the creative act and the noncreative act. Why should there be? Imagination makes life rich and reveals more of what's really here.

Many traditions conceive that after death, the spirit leaves the body — whether to a world beyond or to another body, some passing of time occurs in the intermediate space. The same might be true as we sleep. If so, then a passing spirit or a dozing companion could witness what I do. In the same way that many people read the presence of omens and animal signs, it is valuable to be conscious of the possibility that the imagination forms a real connection. I would get to be a messenger for a while, for someone or something. I would want the omens that I give out to be good ones.

What I form from the imagination depends on my causes and conditions. The imagination wants my actions to be those of self-purification, because the world is an offering. The universe was created — and is being created — as an open-ended act. The best actions strive toward self-improvement without self-interest. These actions are based on duty — not necessarily worldly duty, but not in denial of worldly duty; they extend from your resonance as an image of being.

Once formed in writing, a path has been laid. And a path is a big help for getting somewhere.

## WHAT WOULD YOU DO IF YOU KNEW YOU WOULD FAIL?

Earth is huge. The solar system is huge. The galaxy is huge. And the galaxy is only one of many. You can take a look at the span of time and see our lifespan as the tiniest blip of a moment. Billions of years have passed since the sun was born. Billions more will pass, and the sun will supernova and, with it, Earth will certainly go.

Of all that we can do, it can't last forever. Viewed from a safe distance, the sun's supernova will look beautiful.

We are in the middle of a fascinating paradigm, because although our grandest ambitions will not last forever in precisely the forms we intend, they, with everything, will go on and on as energetic phenomena.

> The point in life is to know what's enough — why envy those otherworld immortals? With the happiness held in one inch-square heart you can fill the whole space between heaven and earth.
>
> — GENSEI

# THE 463 EXERCISE

When circumstances causes me to feel too much self-stuff (importance, anxiety, etc.), I imagine a person very much like myself, thinking very similar thoughts, but this person is living in the year 463. Unlucky for that guy, his time is long gone. Not much that we're now aware of happened in the year 463. The year 463 and all of its inhabitants do not carry their name into the present time.

It may very well be that the current year will, in the distant future, be very similar to the year 463. Spring far enough into the future and maybe that's true. We find the most interest in the current year when we're in it. Because it's here, it will pass, and so let's experience what it means to be alive, plainly, more than striving to hold on to what can't be held but instead holds us.

I breathe and feel my heart beat. I close my eyes and listen to the sound of breath within. I feel and listen for the center point of the inner ear. I locate it first it as a ringing, and I also feel it as a vibration in the center of the head, which follows the pulse of movements that signifies I am alive.

The ability to experience at all is a precious gift. And, wow: I have been given a separate sense of self. Abiding in this state of being, what actions am I drawn to perform? With this state, I have the ability to think and sense: to write.

Sensing the limitations that come from being a self changes my expectations of my practice. Life accrues meaning and fullness, and the fear of failure departs the same way as overlarge expectations of permanent results. Committed to practicing in the present moment, always returning to this intent, I experience freedom within a unique path. The circumstances outside my control neither limit me nor increase or decrease my potential for fulfillment.

# NOTHING IS
## <u>NEW</u>

Doing the impossible (creating something new) is different for everyone because we are differently skilled and motivated. The challenge is one thing; how we react to the challenge is another. When I am beyond my realm of expertise and comfort zone, being proactive is hard.

We hold ourselves back by justifying our challenges and perceived shortcomings. No one wants to spend years struggling with an issue only to find that the solution has been right before him all along. We want a reason for why we're struggling — and often we would rather justify the reason we're struggling than search for the solution. For example, if a writing marathon feels like I am going on and on without the words coming out in the exact form I would expect in a finished manuscript, I may criticize the approach, or criticize something about my abilities. Rather than feeling uncertain, I want to find something to feel right about.

I can't emphasize that point enough: It's confusing to simply stay in uncertainty. So we rationalize things, perhaps as an attempt to make sense of things, even if it doesn't line up perfectly with our other beliefs.

One very talented, very experienced writer whom I worked with at a retreat in Italy expressed that her writing felt unguided, like she was "just going on and on." She believed that, unless she knew ahead of time what form to write in, her writing didn't count.

I asked her if she would be willing to read her piece at critique. The group was eager to hear her read the writing she felt uncertain about. In addition to being interested in the kinds of risks she was taking in her work, they also could connect with her experience as a sort of sounding board for relating and clarifying their own efforts. As it turned out, we were all very interested in what she had read and, after a lively discussion, in which we discovered several patterns in the very work she was afraid merely went "on and on," she learned not only that she had good and original material on her hands, but also that she could have created it no other way than by having plodded forward within the marathon. She learned to trust more in her audience's ability to respond to the energy of the created writing.

When someone is nervous on stage, we share his or her nervousness. Really, we just wish that person trusted that the audience wanted him or her to succeed. If the performers could deeply convince themselves that everyone in the audience was there to see them revel in the state of flow, to see them succeed, the audience, too, could relax. As writers, we can think of the act of writing as a kind of performance, in which we give the audience what it deeply wants, which is to see us succeed beyond our wildest concepts. Even if you pick a book off the shelf half-heartedly, expecting it won't be any good, if you open it up and read a bit of it, and it knocks your socks off, you're far happier than if you had merely felt justified. Rejoicing, we are eager to become more of the listener.

The listener is the writer through the mirror of the page, receptive, neither critical nor full of praise. This mirror shows our relationship to our writing. No one wants to feel that gut-achy state of nervousness. For the sake of the pages we fill, the words we use, the time we spend — and for the reader, if not for ourselves — we should set aside the doubt that seeks only to justify shortcomings. The more we give focus to what we love, the less we can be self-conscious about our performance. When in doubt, remind yourself of the position of watching an actor. We want him to succeed and, in a kind of psychic attempt to help, we're generous. We would beam him good vibes and a pat on the back if we could, so that he could focus on where his energy leads. This reader — the imagination — is always offering inspiration.

1. What is today's expression of why you write?

2. If you give attention to doubt, what do you struggle with?

3. What does the imagination love about your writing?

4. Put yourself in the position of several months from now, well after you've completed today's piece of writing. Imagine that it has in every way exceeded your expectations. Describe the writing in no-qualms positive terms, as if you've discovered a piece by someone you respect and admire.

Doing this reflective work is a useful exercise for opening up to what is possible beyond your wildest expectations. Then, having stretched yourself, you may find that what you deeply want is already within your reach. Having strived, you will find it useful to be free of even the best expectations.

# WITHOUT EXPECTATION

**A**n image: The ringing of a bell in suspensionless space. Sound resonates evenly in all directions, inward and outward, unhindered. Not by any other object, not by space, and not by the bell itself.

You are in the position of that bell. Confront that wide openness, that unadulterated, unkinked honesty. The fear of being open beyond my sense of self is greater than my fear of death, because I can think of death as something that happens to me — being who I truly am requires that I am active in precisely the ways I most want to resist.

The more attentive I am, the more I come to recognize that I am that unattached presence in space. I have a name and a job and preferences and a physical body and everything else that I have. But what I have, I've been given, and the more I pay attention to what I am (rather than what I have), the more the image challenges my sense of self in the best of ways.

I mask this fear by limiting my view, attaching myself to ideas and people, and clinging to the matrix of what's familiar. Yet, no matter how successful I am, at the end of life, I will set aside all that I have. I confront this clear and open image as well when I press myself into uncertainty. In a song, or a moment of writing, or during Hatha yoga practice, I may reach something mysterious and fascinating, an image to which I have not been conditioned to react. Curiosity and passion lead me here, and my natural instinct is to reach for an idol of familiar framework. I don't want to feel out of place, or alone, or crazy. I look for security in whatever way I can find — I search for certainty.

Imagine that, during yoga practice, a person is holding a posture for longer than is comfortable. Her body is safe, but she feels unsteady. Feelings arise, and she feels prone to doing something linguistic with those feelings, like give herself a label. Perhaps she identifies with being a failure, and that label gives her some security by attaching to an internal object, a word, or a belief. Or, perhaps she blames her teacher, and she assigns her sensation to an external object. She wants to write something, but she chooses instead not to write, because she is attached to the certainty that she doesn't have anything to write about, or it wouldn't be any good, or it wouldn't come out right the first time. It gives us a bit of security, but it makes us suffer.

The practice of free-form writing asks that we get rid of these senses of security. When we release false sources of security, we make room for what is already there to be expressed. We feel love and something abundant beyond love. We feel how spacious and sufficient the present moment is, and what a gift it is to be alive, to have the opportunity to make the world a better place, to make art, to be aware, to live as this specific human being, whoever that might be.

Relaxing into that openness, into the support of spaciousness, we are most free to live fully and to act in a way that naturally expresses who we are, which goes beyond our own capabilities for knowing.

Deeply feeling that openness, simply being present to what is before us, something happens, and we feel supported after all. In the overwhelming and awesome spaciousness of pure being (a place with no name to confirm our existence), we can relax and realize we have lost nothing. We are not our moment-to-moment collection of sensations and beliefs. They depart with the movement of time. We are also not our actions. They are the expression of cause and effect for which we are most responsible. We do not need to be partial to what we understand to be the self. Our self-shape enables us to be as we are and practice as we can. But we are not that shape, and the ego is not the doer. Through the practice of poetry, we can overcome the self and then be enabled to function as our own best friend rather than as our own obstacle and enemy.

All this self-shaping is happening to us on some level all the time. The Tibetans believe that within each second there are 600 opportunities to experience self-realization. This internal battle is noticeable when we encounter something new, before we're even able to exclaim or remark internally. When writing, we discover a freshness or an intricacy in each image, which at first may feel too large or too small to conceptualize. The unsupported image offers no comfort or familiarity.

We cling tightly to what we think we have, whether it's valuable or not. We need to know who we are and where we are, but the ego is blind, and so we must admit that it does not always know what is best. When we train it not to be motivated by the fruits of action (or the fruits of inaction), the ego releases its grip on steering toward what justifies it and away from what threatens it, and there becomes room to experience something really wonderful.

Look for the unsupported image in ordinary thoughts, sensations, and events, and you'll find it everywhere. Finding it wholeheartedly, you'll be overwhelmed with a feeling of devotion and compassion. When you feel pressed beyond your comfort zone, just beyond your range of expertise, you are moving toward a divine experience to which you should open yourself. It is a place you cannot go expecting results. Going there, you lose the purpose that led you there.

# THE PLACE THAT TRIMS THE WOOL

Criticism is fine when it's in the proper place, which is afterward. Then, be as critical as you can be and don't try to fool anyone. Put yourself in a place so critical that you recognize that fooling anyone would be failure. That place trims the wool away from the eyes.

The main obstacle to doing what's right is self-interest. The critical wisdom that transcends this urge is coming to understand that we don't always know what's best for us. We are part of a whole, and the more we come to recognize that, the more we naturally offer what is ours to give. Recognizing yourself in others, you naturally respond to their needs. As we come to better understand ourselves, we also come to understand the needs of others as sometimes being not in their best interest. Learning more about ourselves, we also are forced to admit the limits of our knowledge and, as such, we must admit that we cannot fully say what is best in all cases for all people.

Yoga philosophy provides the answer to why most people fear public speaking worse than death. From the standpoint of the ego, authentic expression requires integrity that reaches beyond our comfort zone (and challenges our self-concept).

> For him who has conquered himself by the Self,
> The Self is a friend;
> But for him who has not conquered himself,
> The Self remains hostile, like an enemy
>
> — *Bhagavad Gita* (VI:6)

The author-self concept is good when it's overcome. I associate the author-self with a given persona — coffee drinker, wry, prone to depression — and it behooves me to open beyond this limited view. Strange that it should be hard. Even the appearance of the divine is something we can fear worse than death. Just catching a glimpse of a divine experience through our practice can be deeply unsettling.

When in a writing marathon, we have to move forward. Sometimes we fight the desire to stop and rest. And sometimes we fight the desire to be continually in the flow of things. Often we're cautious to confront something that we close ourselves off to, either by numbing out or by holding the pose by force of will — in either case, losing the ability to be present and aware without judging, allowing the experience to flow through us.

There's no way to "win" at writing. Even being really productive or great with words may not lead to a more intense experience. If it's easier for you to do things a certain way, you will probably want to challenge that, to shake it loose and always be riding just beyond the edge of your experience. That's where growth happens.

Push yourself too far, and you risk weirdness, exhaustion, and perhaps even disillusionment — taking on the wrong stuff or more than you're ready for. Don't push yourself enough, and you're likely to find a false sense of comfort or esteem, a pride that isn't perhaps warranted.

In some sects of ancient Tantra, groups of practitioners would gather in a room to meditate, and then their guru would bring into the room an object of extreme desire. The guru would instruct the meditators to watch. After enough time had elapsed for the meditators' attention to get thoroughly hooked and entangled, the object of their desire would be removed, and they would be told to resume meditation. On one hand, they would have brought an intensity into their meditation that could be very useful. On the other hand, the practice hadn't been built up to deal with such a thing, to balance it out. In other words, the meditators hadn't first cultivated a strong sense of nonattachment. There wasn't so much ground to stand on with the additional energy from viewing the object of their desire. These tantric sects eroded not long after they had been practiced, but these exercises relate to stories that occur to us every day. When beginning a piece of writing, we may project expectations about the finished work. It can be built up too much before it has even taken form.

Continual practice is hard. To help overcome the pride of such a practice, I make sure I keep myself just beyond the edge of my own expertise. To help balance out the sense of shame that can arise from constantly feeling challenged, I do what I can to remind myself of the increased rewards brought by the practice, and reaffirm that I am open to feel whatever is necessary to achieving freedom and growth. And I let the feelings — good or bad — flow through me rather than finding sticky resonance against an internal story.

Any practice that takes a person away from the ordinary and exposes her to a wealth of its own concepts, terms, and traditions will feel different or foreign. It's important to transcend the duality of different or same, and instead consistently serve a personal truth.

You may have some fear of taking a class or of going on a retreat that differs in some way from what you're used to; then, having braved the experience, you may have some fear of returning to the community. This fear often turns into a false embrace, in which it becomes important that, upon returning to the community, we are seen as different than before, as significant from everyone else. There are times when it's best to stand up for one's beliefs, and there are other times when to do so would be offensive, either for one's environment or with respect to how the beliefs are being conveyed — perhaps as a totem or achievement, when, in fact, the truth only emerges through actual lived experience, and not by being recognized by others as being one way or the other.

> ◢ *You feel different because of the experience and more the same because of the truth.*
>
> — Yoganand Michael Carroll

I look in a mirror and see the visual reflection of my body at a given time. I look into the mirror a moment later and see roughly the same image, unless I've made some dramatic change to my appearance. I look into the mirror a third, fourth, fifth time, and the pattern that tends to emerge is that I won't necessarily see myself each moment; instead, I am basically just being reminded of what I already know.

It's good that things persist, because that resolution allows us to grow and improve the more we practice. It's good also to know that we often take for granted that things are the same when, in fact, nothing is really exactly the same from one moment to the next. Some food that your body is digesting has made its way a little farther through your system. Your heartbeat has been doing its thing; you've taken new breaths. What doesn't seem important to us gets rounded off into a place we open up to when practicing poetry or yoga.

Imagine looking into a mirror and also seeing the images of how you looked years ago, how you'll look in the distant future. Which one is the right representation of you? Is it truer as you proceed, or are you moving away from the soulful representation of you?

For a while we persist, but after an indeterminate length of time, we no longer do so. The length of time won't really matter when the moment of death approaches. Our achievements won't matter when death reaches us. Life is beautiful beyond its temporal limitations. We can achieve realization and a sense of overwhelming oneness even in our lifetime. We can put ourselves to work today, as living, breathing, healthy people.

What we give away openly, we experience fully, and what we hang onto, we lose. We fight ourselves crazy to lock our sense of self into an imaginary stasis. There was a man who liked broccoli but he didn't like kale. Thursdays, when it was cooked, he liked cauliflower, but he never liked cauliflower on Fridays, or cauliflower and broccoli mixed — ever. That was when he was eight

— he had at least that much figured out. He turned eighteen and, as time passed, he figured out a lot of other things, like how to drive a car, how to apply for a job, how to parasail, and one day he realized he was relishing cauliflower and broccoli and kale, whether it was Thursday or they were cooked or raw, together, or separate. To him there seemed to be no contradiction.

Our need to feel certain and self-consistent is by habit extremely strong; it takes a deep practice to loosen our grip on the constraints of self-representation. In return, we can embrace the openness of spontaneity. We can come to trust nature, inside and out.

We're doing that kind of emotional jiu-jitsu all the time to stay self-consistent. We change from moment to moment, hopefully living in a way that increases our sense of fullness and meaning in life. The moments roll forward, and we can use the regularity of material occurrence, the persistence of matter, to progress in our practice.

Whenever we're not curious, interested, engaged, receptive to experience, when we shut down and wish for nature to be some other way, we're fighting an impossible battle, and we're only creating pain. This pain can manifest within us in the form of emotional tightness and psychological rigidity. It can lead to arguments and bitterness with others whom we relate to, and to mistrust of those we have as yet only imagined meeting — potential friends and acquaintances. We do all this work to stay self-consistent. In reality, everything (including us) is far more interesting and various than we could ever fully conceive.

Understanding first that things just *are* can liberate us from unhealthy self-consistency by returning us to the undying curiosity that engages us with the world beyond our concept of self.

It doesn't matter how long we've spent forming a cohesive world-view that trains our conscious mind to appraise the success of our self-concept. What's inside is more important. We can get at it from the outside as well: entering the forest firsthand, exploring the multitude of independently moving sights, the smells of life, the dark environment's breeze and chatter.

The truth is that you're on a path already. Pursue love's deepest expression to such an extent that nothing is left over, no sense of self. All that you do and think are offerings, expressions of the divine paid back to the divine. Appearances are relative — they change with perspective, with time, and with mood. Through all potential appearances is the experience of authentic being. Let that move you.

You have the ability to move around. When something doesn't suit you, when the situation is uncomfortable, you can change things. Not everything has latitude. Many plants, for example, have very little latitude. A collection of moss growing on the side of a stone has no say over whether the workings of rain cause it to tumble down and get buried. As humans, we always have some latitude.

In writing, I have the ability to alter my perspective so that I am more playful and involved. I am free with regard to how I use my latitude. What brought me to the page asks only that I continue to honor the call.

I trust my practice. When I know that what I am doing poses no real risks, I face an irrational fear. That is the ego's irrational fear of opening into the knower.

Intrinsically, by nature, we are free. Even at this very moment, we are free. As full of the baggage or worries or doubt that circumstances might hand us, through all the perceptible clues of baggage, we are actually free.

In this practice, many things call for your attention. The call you should answer depends on the moment, and the only way to know is by practicing discernment. More than anything else, you must cultivate a sensitive internal witness. It is central that you do not become attached to feelings or meanings, and instead practice openly, with what might be considered restraint — restraint from the expectation of choosing what you receive. The practice of absolute devotion affirms with trust that you are open to feel what the divine causes you to feel. It may be confusing, it may be blissful beyond comparison, and it may feel icky. It is good to let these things pass. And, anyway, they're only true for that moment, after which if we hold onto them they become something else — they become a story. The mind speaks in words. The ego speaks in feelings and is always assessing the elements of perception for well-being or threat. The more you practice with integrity of devotion, the more your ego will be challenged, so it is crucial that you work to cultivate a strong ability to discern, to be acutely attentive.

There are a million games the ego can play, a million ways of forming stories from the elements of sense perception. I may feel that I deserve the feelings of blissful practice and go around feeling entitled. I may own the weird feelings of turmoil brought up by practice, believing that I am in some way flawed. I may be tempted to set aside practice altogether out of the threat it poses to the ego. I am certainly overwhelmed by the extent to which I construct stories out of what initially is "just" sensation.

# DELAYED GRATIFICATION: TEMPERATURE RISING

In ancient Sankya practice, it was believed that by denying the senses of gratification, you burned them. This is to be taken as a sacrificial rather than a literal fire. For this reason, after they died, advanced yogis were not cremated, but buried, because cremation was a means of purifying the body to ready it for rebirth elsewhere. The yogi was one who had burned himself, his senses, burned out his impurities in this life, and it was fitting to simply bury him in the ground. There is the saying that a realized person resembles a burnt thread — at the slightest touch of wind, he dissolves entirely.

In practice, you metaphorically offer your senses actions that challenge and purify them. After your practice, you become a more open person, one whose senses reveal what is truly there, at the slightest touch — pure being, inside and out. Through language, you offer your mind a kind of sacrificial fire that opens you to a more direct experience of truth.

Many, many years ago, Vedic priests would construct "chariots," perhaps signified by a careful outlining of rice, in which they would (ritually) fly to the sun. As yoga came more onto the scene, the imagery persisted, and the sun came to be understood as something else, namely the energies in the belly. Yoga enabled practitioners to yoke the sun in the belly through ways of posturing the body and focusing the mind and controlling breath. Subtle energy that normally engaged with the outlets of activities could be generated and allowed to circulate more freely. Rays from the sun came to be understood as *nadis* or energy channels inside. No priest was needed. Energy itself became the teacher. In a similar way, yoga reaches me in my writing practice. It is very important to recognize that yoga takes many forms, inward and outward, and it is good to keep an open mind regarding issues of achievement about things that are difficult or sometimes impossible to see, even within the self.

The highest posture in yoga, as put forth by the *Bhagavad Gita*, is sitting in lotus posture performing *kichari mudra*. From the outside, the posture might not reveal its own level of achievement — and that should be remembered.

So what is *kichari mudra*? When the body's prana (aliveness) is high enough, when the energies have been churned through practice, the witness has been trained as a renunciate, and the mind is ready to receive, the kundalini (sometimes referred to by Swami Kripalu as the "menace of kundalini") energy rises up the spine. The yogi is able to do so because all the nervous system's channels of energy have been opened and purified. The body has been trained to trust yoga practice above all else, and the energy spontaneously rises up the central channel of the spine (the shushumna nadi), overwhelming all other sense functions. The tongue, under the direction of prana, presses hard into the roof of the mouth and ascends into the nasal cavity, experiencing the spaciousness at that center point in the middle of the head, the realm of heaven in Hindu mythology. The tongue in this position is *kichari mudra*. Getting the tongue there takes practice — ordinarily, the tendon prevents anything close to such movement, but through practice it has been stretched. The tongue is pressed there to help direct more energy toward the metaphorical realm of heaven. The combination of heightened prana and the tongue creates the mudra and the experience — simply cutting the tendon and moving one's tongue into this position would not be the same thing.

In this position, the tongue is pressed near the opening of the nasal cavity, merging sensations of feeling, scent, taste, and hearing, the tongue's tip moved toward the third eye, this central point. And, perhaps, what the eye sees is the thousand-petaled lotus.

The practice of nada yoga can, in effect, be thought of as visualization for this practice. It may be of some help toward achieving this physical phenomenon and will remain a rich visualization with its own rewards. What happens on an energetic or spiritual level can be difficult to measure. The unstruck sound can be thought of as the sweet music of dissolving, or *laya*. I believe it makes for better writing to draw attention there, to the space in the center from which the single sound that exists in all things emanates.

# STRUCTURES
# THAT BRING
# OUT THE BEST
# IN YOU

**T**he word dharma can mean many things. One of the more useful meanings is *the structure that brings out your best.*

Each of us has a unique connection to dharma, so it's just as important to be sensitive to our response to any given practice as it is to learn everything we can about them. The structure that brings out the best in you is unique. You can relay it to other people, and they will be able to connect with what you share based on two primary things: the specific aspects that you mention, and your physiological integration with what you're saying — the extent to which you are able to mean what you're saying.

When I trod along the path of writing, for example, and I share it with my friends, telling people how wonderful it is and all that it's done for me, other people might be able to relate to what I am saying. They also might be able to relate to the way I am saying it, regardless of their experience with writing, and they may fill in the blanks with metaphors that connect to their direct experience — perhaps of their connection to their own goals, and perhaps based on their intuition for these things. One person's evangelism might open doors for other people. It is good to know that there is some relativity in these matters, and to be nonjudgmental. Is it better, for example, that one person is pursuing yoga full time at an ashram somewhere? Maybe. It is possible, unfortunately, that doing so might not lead to the right place — whether the teacher is not right, or the practice is confused, or perhaps something else should be worked out beforehand. Following anyone else's way will not lead me to my relationship with truth. In my practice, I do the best I can to find metaphors with other ways I have found, and I do my best to be sensitive to the nuances of my practice, which the deepest part of me knows must be followed.

Yoganand Michael Carroll once told the story of a bit of travel he had done in India. He said that one morning, he and a few of his friends left in a van to visit a waterfall, and on their way through the city, they passed a man in his front yard holding himself in the headstand posture. The headstand is often thought to be a difficult pose, and so those who do the pose or have some experience with it might feel a certain way about someone else who is able to arrive at some perfection within the pose. Yoganand and his friends continued in their van and went on to spend the day at the waterfall and do other sightseeing. On their way back, late in the evening, they passed through the same town and, again, saw the man in his yard, still holding himself in a headstand. It was admirable that he could hold the posture for such a long time, but — Yoganand wondered — why did he choose to do it in his front yard?

It's understandable to want to show off your skills. But when a practice is intended to be one of personal significance, it's misplaced to look outside for praise. To obtain balance, it is said that one should live in different modes depending on where you find yourself. In the world, one should follow Vishnu, the protector and sustainer. In the solitude of yoga, one should follow Siva, god of renunciation and transformation. Within the self, one should follow Shakti, wild fertile goddess of life.

This means that you want to be a good person in the world, following the path of nonviolence, ethics, and responsibility. Sometimes you will need to follow the law, and sometimes your heart will speak that the general momentum of society is troublesome, and our social habits will need to improve. The real authority here is the middle way, always middling between two and unity, multiples and singular.

In your practice, you want to renounce the world in a practical sense by separating yourself for a time from worldly relations and responsibilities; also by creating a place where you can focus entirely on the spirit, which means setting aside preconceived notions. This practice also means expressing devotion that does not expect a receipt, practicing because it is the heart's expression, because it is the right thing to do. This kind of practice will do it for free.

Inside, you want to be energetically free. On the outside, the total free play of energy would be monstrous. But inside, it's healthy. Who can know all that your electrons are doing, and who can count the various multiplications of your cells, the pumping of blood that is just right for you to live? Taking a step forward or a step back, we see that the way of nature is for boundless freedom. Inside, you want your cells to know the vitality of freedom. This entails doing the kind of work only someone wholeheartedly willing to renounce the fruits of labor should do. Someone who has not properly developed the ability to maintain sensitivity and mindfulness would risk getting lost in even a touch of what really is boundless freedom, though, even a glimpse of boundless freedom can have immensely positive effects and can help the world in tremendous ways.

Your practice is a unique structure that brings out the best in you. A touch of honey against the tongue is worlds away from even the best description of honey. Both are good.

# IMAGE-
## MARRIAGE

The field and the knower of the field are intimately entwined. The ground beneath your feet is real. Also, the ground beneath your feet changes as you move. Your ground is the ground of your experience. Building sensitivity and awareness in your practice, you come to know consciousness as the force you are opening to, the force to which you offer the fruits of your actions.

Practicing, one retraces the path of creation back to the source. In a personal sense, practicing is self-realization, coming to know the extent of what you can truly know. In a deeper sense, practicing is also coming to know the self, or pure and unattached awareness, above, within, and beneath consciousness; the breath of life commingling with the material manifestations of life.

The experience of pure awareness reminds us of the lack of separation between consciousness and matter. We come to realize that we're not simply experiencing the sensation of breath, but that there are sensations for breath. There is a concept of a persistent self that experiences and manages those sensations. Gradually, as we practice, our brain forms patterns among the elements of sense perception, and we gain familiarity with categories and manifestations.

I am in a cabin in the woods. It's early in the morning. I take a step outside and breathe in the fresh air, listen to the birds, hear the light breeze brushing the trees. I am in nature. I step back inside the cabin, feel the floorboards underfoot, hear the humming of the refrigerator motor, the low buzz of the laptop computer, the various silences brought about by the arrangement of rooms, the smell of food in the kitchen. I am still in nature — indoors, but still in nature.

Nature is absolutely everything. The far reaches of the void of outer space — the sum total of human experience, the gurgle of digestion in your belly. It is enlightening to see everything as part of nature.

I am most certainly not the inventor. At the same time, I do get to put myself into the place of the inventor. Each time I write, it is being done in a way that has never happened before in all of history, and will never be done again in just the same way. This instant of experience is precious.

I recognize in the experience that I am grateful that I get to do it. Allowed to practice yoga, understanding what I do, I am open to what can reveal itself to me today. Moving words and phrases around, I choose amidst the freedom of feelings to be flooded with devotion.

Afterward, in my daily life, I carry the memory of this devotion as an energy that flows through my cells. Encouraging my cells to remember the flood of devotion, I accomplish the impossible.

# IMAGES THAT
# REVERBERATE

t is useful to keep in mind that language is a natural phenomenon. Though I do not always think in words, I do make use of them, and they guide my attention. I am surrounded by nature. I am nature. Nature is inside, too. Everything I can touch or imagine is part of nature. Language offers a path through the use of words, which symbolize concepts, senses, and relations.

Language accrues significance through the use of metaphors. Using language figuratively has an effect, and a wonderful thing about language is that the effects can be numerous. A more musical style of writing engenders a musical appreciation and interaction with the language, not pressuring words so much on their literal meaning. It's more of an interaction and play of sounds ordered by thought through time. The landscape of language is as diverse as nature. The more attentive I am as a writer, the more I invite the reader to engage with language.

Along the path of language created by the words the writer uses, words serve as images — not necessarily limited to visual phenomena, but including the full spectrum of cognitive and sense experience.

An image is the representation of a thing. The invocation of the word "cactus" brings all the potentials for the word "cactus," as well as all your connotations for the word, which are influenced by every aspect of the moment that carries the word to you — its rhythm, the words surrounding it, the language of your immediate experience, the circumstances, your biology, and the entirety of your history and conditioning. When it is said that everything has already been written, that nothing is new under the sun, the potential truth of that phrase cannot alter the significance of this present moment for you as a lived one.

An image can also be the embodiment or enactment of a state or feeling, as can happen through the image's resonance with the surrounding language environment. The mention of a rose amid descriptions of a grave might, for example, be poeticizing the mystery of life's end, the struggles for meaning that seem impossible to understand and yet can surprise us with monstrous beauty — monstrous because it does not obey any laws or rules. On the other hand, the same invocation of the word *rose* in stuttering syllables by a lover to one whom he hopes is his beloved conveys something else, which we might say is a kind of life-affirming adoration.

An image is a metaphor with you. Through its reverberation, any image can enact the experience of pure being. The Sanskrit phrase *tat tvam asi* ("you are that") is an example — and it is direct. It may be meaningful to take this phrase as a template for direct observation, which takes into account the role of managing what one is attentive to, and, simultaneously, the way in which one is attentive. Paying attention to a rose and noticing its naivety or noticing its overwhelming beauty depends entirely on one's attention. Both possibilities are expressed, not, perhaps, because of the flower but because of the nature of attention. Depending on how it strikes you, the reading experience can bring a moment of awakening.

Through improved attention arises the understanding of nature as wild, unbounded, all-encompassing — with this perspective, a balanced and sustainable life of spontaneity, creativity, and generosity makes sense, and the balanced life is anything but simple.

# 6. BALANCE

# BALANCE: THE WORKING LIFE

An enriched creative process requires both time and intensity. I cannot multitask and create a work of singular beauty; putting myself fully into the creative process means letting all else fall away.

History overflows with well-known individuals who have accomplished more than they could have dreamed. History doubly overflows with powerful, dynamic, wonderful individuals whose great mission and quest in life saw its fulfillment, whether they achieved any sort of fame or even recognition.

As our population grows and our social networks change, the structure of reputation is also changing. Ours is a rapidly expanding culture with many movements. These categories emerge organically (through community consent) and with individual assertion (by coining/marketing a unique niche). In light of this expanding-universe model, branches of the market tree grow increasingly nuanced and numerous. There is a place for everyone to be authentic.

When doing anything of significance, we make a break from our existing community. Community seeks to stabilize the members belonging to it. Just as we seek harmony within ourselves, each of us within a community seeks to establish harmony among community members. When people are out of line, the community can round them out and get them back into a place where they're harmonious.

We need to be on the lookout for where these departures from the norm are potentially positive forces, so that we can be encouraging. One person can help shift the balance of a community toward a more positive place, but that person's efforts only find traction when many others get involved.

Most communities are self-organizing systems. Instead of having a leader, they have fluidity of power exchange. Within the self, we work the same way. We order ourselves not by a single authoritarian declaration but by our averaged-out habits and actions, our relationships, and by the way we live each day. We aren't in competition with a whole mass of people to get to the top of a hierarchical pyramid. Instead, we are each our own pyramid, and we are only in competition with ourselves.

When we leave one community, we find another. When there isn't another community, we aren't alone in the space where one may emerge. There are always forces at work in our lives. The task before each human is to enter the dark woods and go the way he or she must. Confronting another way may be helpful but it probably isn't your way. Opportunities present themselves in the untrodden darkness of the forest, because nature is boundless in her ability to inspire and compel. We are always in touch with the boundless; when living in harmony with nature, you know you are in touch with the boundless.

The rest of the world does not need to change before I need to do my work as an individual. Truth gives me the only valuable thing, which is a life of integrity, curiosity, and awe.

It's noteworthy to mention the different concept we have now of the word *genius*. Nowadays, we refer to someone as a genius, by which we mean that he or she is brilliant. The historical use of the word has been a little different, and the difference is worth mulling over —particularly to reflect on how we relate to the ownership of ideas. Traditionally, it was said that someone's genius was such-and-such, more as a synonym for disposition or spirit — as in, it's Stephen's genius to write prose poems. It's what Stephen does because that's the genius he relates to. By shifting how we relate to this word, we can be a lot freer and make things that express a life well lived.

# REVISE WITH GOOD HEART

Sometimes what gets written is clear and good and doesn't need or ask for further revision. You don't need to clarify anything, you don't need to add or subtract anything. As it was written in the first place, so it will stand, and its greatest truth will be honored. You may as well have just gone ahead and carved it into stone that way.

And sometimes it's necessary to re-enter work, retrod the path — to honor what works, to further flesh out what remains hidden or unrealized. Rereading something, time has passed, and we have changed — our perspective has changed, we have been exposed to other things; we are removed from the spell invoked at the time in which we wrote the piece. You may revisit the work minutes later — or maybe years. What we can achieve in retouching that expression, the form made by our relationship to that moment, is the stuff of revision.

When weeding a garden, we have no need to obsess over what has been pulled out. Our real focus, though our hands are busy with undesirables, is on what we want to live there. After all, in the garden and on the page, whether something is a weed is a matter of opinion.

It takes real work to reenter the magic and spirit of a piece of writing. It will go much more smoothly and even be enjoyable when we're open-hearted about the whole thing. It may even come to be the most enjoyable time for working. Musical artists often really enjoy the overdubbing and layering part because the main track has been laid down. Writing a novel, we may find it a relief to have made it through the story, to have worked out all the structural and character nuances, all the plot points, to have resolution more or less recorded there on the page.

We all have favorite parts of the creative process. I like the first draft. I particularly like being just a tad bit into it. There is the beginning of a path; a fresh imaginative landscape has just begun to be revealed. It's my job to keep things fresh and relate to that freshness.

It is useful to know what aspects I like, because it helps to expand my adoration into a new area. The real reason for a good understanding of what motivates us (and how to get motivated for what is truly our life's work) is that the thing itself is always changing its outward form. What appeals to me one day may completely change in a few years' time.

Lucky for us, we don't need to know everything about what we're doing. But we do need to be in love with the soulful particulars. Your work should be the thing you can turn to when everything else in life gets you down. It may demand more from you than anything else, but you turn to it because it holds more rewards than anything else.

The rewards are not external. Your practice may just not be one that the market will pay for. That doesn't mean it isn't valuable, or that we only pay for what we deem valuable. We are all stopped in our steps at a glimpse of beauty, at the slightest revelation of the sublime.

I like to think of revision as a kind of re-entry into the precise moments of creation in which, after the fact, having more experience inside the work, the writer can be sensitive, providing support and scaffolding to the moments that need it, energy to those that feel stretched or thin, and cut the things that feel forced or untrue, rather than the things that seem merely out of place.

Revision — think of it as retouching — is best done without too much thinking. Too much editing, in the imaginative sense, puts off the inevitable. It makes us healthier as artists to affirm what we do, and when we overcome the desire to make things appear tidier than imaginatively presented, we're making it harder for ourselves in the future to be able to trust spontaneity.

I'm emphatic about this idea, because all too often, I see in the assertion of bad energy the life of the piece (its wildness, its unpredictability, its funky moments) gets erased, as it feels daunting to relate to something at that energetic level. A fundamental challenge with being creative comes in forming something innovative or new and helpful or entertaining or surprising: to know that the real writing happens in the moment — that moment in which we first fill the page with words and the extended moment of revision, the re-entry into the work.

Revision is also the opportunity to return to fundamentals, and to simplify. Because revision happens after the fact, it becomes possible to study one's fundamentals of phrasing, of word choice, of prose rhythm, and to engage in a bigger analysis of your work's arguments and motifs. Revision can be entropic, leaving an emergent pattern, like the ripples left in sand when the waves pass over.

Sometimes upon revisiting work, the brain forms new shorthand and patterns to map the landscape. When I think of the created material as having been sung to me in its precise moment, and I see myself as the editor choosing to remove those moments, it's possible that in an energetic sense, I am removing the opportunities presented to me by the imagination throughout time, and making that abundant window smaller and less meaningful to me. Now is always a good time to make that window larger, to chill out. To maintain a sense of support during the challenge, returning to simple ideas is good, enabling me to remember that I am dealing with layers of sounds presenting themselves as words with which we associate images and forms. Sentences — what marvels — can be phrased in ways that convey certain emotional and musical truths. A short phrase reads differently than a long and winding interrupted phrase. A sentence that suspends comprehension by placing information necessary to the reader's concept of the subject toward the end has a certain feeling. Revision is an opportunity to slow down and rethink our use of images and words. The way we choose to do it is the right one when it challenges us, serves the listener, and feels fun.

It is good to know what you want, and I've found it most helpful at the revision stage to have a clear sense for the story emotionally, if not yet rationally. That way, I'm not limiting myself in any formal sense; instead, I'm expressly guided toward the completion of an affecting picture or relationship. I know when the story is finished because of how it feels. The great thing about creative work is that when something has meaning for me, it can also have meaning for someone else.

# EXERCISE: REVISION AND POLISHING MARATHON

For this exercise, begin a new writing marathon using material you've already generated. This is a good opportunity to make several passes through the written piece and to revise it.

- Read each sentence and consider that the feeling/information could be phrased differently. Can it be phrased better?
- Can the chapters better frame the tension-and-release?
- Should the paragraphs do the same work as chapters in miniature?
- Do you want the story's beginning to hook the listener's interest?
- Does the first 1/3 provide raised stakes that reward her investment? Does it need to?
- Does the middle draw her into the heart of the work?
- Does the story conclude in a way that amazes the listener?

# MARKETING

Once you have written your piece, you may want to spread the word about it. This entails marketing. Marketing is within reach of everyone who is passionate about the subject, style, or genre of writing, because to be successful, all you have to do is reach people directly based on a shared interest. You don't need to broadcast your message to the whole world. Instead, "narrowcast" your message authentically to the right people (people like you), and you'll find an eager audience ready and waiting.

The main marketing problem I have had as an author is a psychological one. I will sputter around rather than effectively conveying the value of my own stuff. It's true that the best resource is resourcefulness, and when I really am inspired and have an unstoppable belief about something, I see it through to completion. Any limiting belief with regard to self-confidence or work ethic has a detrimental effect on marketing.

Secondly, you need to believe in your writing, and you need your belief to connect to a vision or mission. The more responsible you feel for the care you have put into the finished product, the more motivated you'll be to sell its value to others.

Marketing has been hugely rewarding, because it has enabled me to connect with amazing people who are interested in the same kinds of things I am. That said, it's also been a challenge, and I wish I'd had the information I'm sharing with you when I was getting started.

It's important simply to remember that marketing is a way of empowering ourselves to connect with other people. When you believe in what you're doing, it really is as simple as the desire to share something of value with others.

To this end, I would recommend finding as many ways as you can to keep yourself accountable — not merely "on track" but in an upward momentum fueled by your passion. And make sure that your friends and loved ones know you want their support to keep you accountable. It will help to spread outward from a circle of support, and you deserve to have that assistance.

Because the structure of publishing has changed, authors today take on more of the marketing responsibility even when they are publishing a book through traditional means. It helps to see marketing as an organic extension of the creative process. It comes down to being authentic and conveying what you really have to offer.

Speak from your authentic voice directly to your devoted fans. The more you focus yourself and speak passionately to specific groups of people, the more effective your communication will be. Remember that there are real human beings out there who would love to come across what you're sharing. As an extension of your mission, start a blog or contribute to a journal and start writing about what you love. Make connections with other people based on a mutual interest.

It's almost always necessary to build up a fanbase before you start selling anything, but remember that, in the end, it's easy to give people what they want. We all love to support people who offer something valuable. Nonetheless, imagining that as a reality can still be hard when I myself am in that position — but I do it, and it does work.

For his whole life, Walt Whitman was his own evangelist. Really putting your heart and soul into your writing and sharing that love and connecting with others is a reward in itself. Beyond connecting with good writing, the reader connects with your engagement. We all love to be close to someone who is open and in love and thriving.

This entails generating quality material and giving it away. It's hard to make friends when you have a product in front of you, but it's easy to sell something when you already have a following. You build a following by being authentic and generous. Not getting the results you wanted? Be more authentic, and be more generous.

With social media, you get to tap into a very efficient form of word-of-mouth marketing. Eben Pagan is an online marketer who often talks about giving away your best ideas rather than keeping them to yourself. He and many other people have had a lot of success by doing exactly this. It can be counterintuitive, but when you give away your best ideas, you tap into the law of reciprocity. When we recognize that we are receiving something valuable, we want to give back. In addition, when you factor social networking in with giving away your best idea, and you make it easy for people to share your information, the process moves a lot more efficiently.

When you're marketing something, you want to have some clarity about where you can find people who share your interests. In marketing terminology, that's your *niche*: the relationship between what you're interested in and what other people want. The more you focus on something much larger than yourself, the easier it is to stay motivated, and you're clearing a space for community based on that passion.

My process starts with a fulfilling practice — a practice that extends to my family and friends, adding value to my life as a happy, fulfilled person, a devoted writer, a great person, and a gardener, and extending further into the world, where I offer my work, connect with others and make friends. I am who I am, so I might as well share that with the world rather than what I think might look better. When I am authentic, people appreciate it. It all circles back to having integrity in my practice. I am giving form to something durable, and so I am patient, staying just beyond the edge of my expertise, and always returning to what I love.

# YOUR WRITING'S
# ROLE

Beyond polishing a book so that you honor its emotional and artistic truth, if you're hoping that the book can serve a purpose or fill a role in the world, or if you want the book to be inspiring or helpful to a specific audience, you need to ensure that the book meets its needs as well. To do that, you can put yourself in the listener's shoes.

In recalling a time you've needed something, you know that you were never as interested in the details of the object you wanted as much as you were aware of your own need. Focus on what your audience needs, and use your creativity to address those needs authentically. Even if your only desire is to be entertaining, the same holds true. The reality is that they may already be actively searching for what you would like to offer.

# THE EDITOR'S "CUT AND GROW" APPROACH

A writing marathon is a direct way to form a tighter allegiance with the creative impulse. The editor with no ego contributes the best of his/her attentive skill while yielding to the direction of the creative impulse. Creativity has no limits, is eternally valuable, and has no means of valuation. Criticism within itself possesses no value other than the ability to assess. When creativity and criticism are combined, a work can be innovative and express its originality. Whether a work is consistently good is often not a question of the quality of the creativity, but — ironically — of the critical drive, insofar as the critical informs and enlarges the creative impulse. It is a marriage. In art, we most appreciate the two making love.

It is good to affirm that there is absolutely no limit to creativity, other than the time supplied toward its expression. Love, intentionally, each part of the process, and write first to please yourself. The critic is the parent voice, the teacher voice, the editor. Gratitude diffuses the editorial ego and puts this persona at the service of the creative impulse.

We have an internal teacher, and if we choose to read our own work with the teacher's mindset, we have a great tool. The editor cannot create, but that's as it should be. In observing, we understand that, because it is limitless, the creative extends beyond us as well.

> *An opened eye finds the poem that carries the poet away.*
> — Donald Revell

The finished product will be better when you move continually forward, neither forcing yourself to go too fast nor moving haltingly, remaining honest and heartfelt. In life, shutting down after a mistake will prevent coming to full terms with the wider story. I cannot pretend to know the story that is larger and truer than the ones I intend to supply for myself to make meaning.

The psychic energy that would have been spent justifying a situation can be channeled toward a clear purpose or left available and free for locating and enlarging a moment of opportunity. I can see myself as the protagonist, but that is artifice. I want to be free of stories. I have everything I need already; the check is in the mail.

> *The branch from which the blossom hangs is neither too long nor too short.*
> — J. Krishnamurti

You're alive! Let yourself be surprised at how fruitful it is to persist for the sake of your best interests. And, at any rate, remember that it's not about the form (what the material looks like); it's about your approach to writing.

# EXERCISE: LOCATE MOTIFS

Read back through the material generated during a writing marathon. Locate the key images and recurring motifs.

Focus on developing the motifs you have located. Give yourself time and focus to weave the motifs back into the story to maintain uniformity of landscape.

For example, if you have noticed that your story features several instances of unpredictable weather, how is that motif affecting the story's pacing? Do you spend enough time describing the snow? Do the characters interact with the weather? How is the weather, as a motif, a character in itself? Notice the magic elements in the scenery. Let the scenery reveal itself as animistic in how things act of their own accord.

# EXERCISE: DISMISSING DEFEAT

It may happen when you feel pressured to write: You don't want to do it. You feel defeated.

In fact, there is this looming possibility: You don't have to write. It isn't impossible that you resolve right here and now never to write again. You might want to pause for a moment and really let the feeling effect you. What would happen if you chose never to write again?

You are a free person, after all, and if you resolved to do it, you could eliminate any possibility that you would ever set pen to paper again or touch a keyboard with the intent to "write." Sure, you might send a quick email or check what's going on in the news. You'd sign a check here and there — or maybe you'd even resolve to stop writing to such a degree that you'd insist someone else did your check writing and your email checking.

It is possible. You could fully and completely stop writing.

If you made that decision, what would happen? Imagine your life. Imagine being the person who never writes anything.

Of the following, who lives most fully?

- the person who writes when he wants to, whether it's good or not
- the person who never writes because he doesn't want to
- the person who sometimes writes when he wants to, and sometimes it doesn't work out

Would you live more fully having renounced writing?

If there's any doubt, you owe it to yourself to examine that doubt, and do whatever is necessary to transcend the doubting.

The purpose of running through this exercise is to carve out more of a deep internal nook, in which you can know your identity for certain. If you have a book in you, you owe it to yourself — and possibly to many others — to write that book. It's nice to be around people who are really doing their soul's work. Forgive yourself for not writing, and don't pressure yourself to write when you don't feel like it. Give yourself full permission to be creative when your intuition says that it's time for you to write.

Give yourself the opportunity to give up writing forever so that procrastination is no longer a temptation. The deeper the decision, the deeper the resulting certainty, the better able you'll be to cope with challenges — imaginative, interpersonal, financial, physical, emotional, and so on. Even just having this one certainty will positively impact other aspects of your being. It's a holistic approach. Resolve one doubt, and another comes (as long there is time and energy to doubt), so be grateful for the ups and downs. The ups and downs, twists and turns, are the expressions of life — something bigger than us — breathing.

# EXERCISE: DEPARTURES

During your next writing session, take seven departures from the main idea, plotline, dominant images, and/or characters. Spend an inordinate amount of time in these seven regions, delighting in the freedom you have in doing so. Keep track of each departure, and return to each at least three times during the progression of your writing session, encouraging the act of weaving back to the departure to show the reader a fresh moment with some similarities to an experience in recent memory.

For example, let's say you're writing a scene in which a man is packing up his belongings, and he drops a snow globe onto the ground, and it breaks. Imagine spending a good amount of time on one nuance of the snow globe — that could be one departure. For a return to this image, let's say you've moved onto a scene in which a husband and a wife are cooking dinner together. Perhaps the husband is rolling out a ball of dough roughly the same size as the snow globe. Describe it in similar terms, attentive to any emotional charge within the image's invocation.

# EXERCISE:
## STORYBOARDING

The three-act structure is intrinsically compelling. We find it in traditions all over the world. It's not the right way for all writing, but it's useful to look to this structure. In the end, each story finds its own structure and shape. The three-act structure is not the most real thing. Stories themselves are where we learn best about structure, and so I have found it best to write more in service of the emergent.

A storyboard is essentially a notecard of information about the structure within a scene. If you have enough storyboards, you can tell the entirety of your story's plot, though not the entirety of a story.

To storyboard an entire book might entail one notecard for each page — when you really include all the details. When you limit yourself in how many storyboards you have to work with, you're forced to isolate the key plot points within your story, which during the process of drafting a book may or may not correspond to the three-act structure. This style of organic book organization arranges your attention evenly among the significant structural elements.

When constructing your storyboards, be attentive to the many shapes of structure. Depending on your lens, you could track protagonist development, antagonist action, major and minor setting changes, charged objects, and the sequential effects of each scene.

1. Fit your story into thirty storyboards.

2. Next, fit your story into thirteen storyboards. Make each storyboard so that it conveys the essentials of your plot.

3. Finally, design seven storyboards to convey the essential progression.

When you know the necessary moments in the necessary order, you can make a hugely helpful revision, because the story has been mapped out. Should you ever be confronted with the feeling that you understand too much about your story, dive into the movement of images.

# DINNER PARTY EXERCISE

Napoleon Hill, author of *Think and Grow Rich*, one of the most innovative books in the field of self-development, came up with a really interesting exercise he would do every day. He was thinking long and hard about ways to overcome challenges and empower others, and he wanted to know what some of history's great minds would think about his ideas, so he would assemble an imaginary collection of deeply inspiring figures in a room in his mind. Each evening, he would spend some time in that imaginary room with his projections of these inspiring people, and before long, he was amazed at how much substantive feedback he received. One of the people he invited to his mastermind group was Abraham Lincoln — because, after all, there weren't any limits to who was able to attend. He reported that these sessions were remarkably centering and deeply inspiring.

I recently started doing this activity as well, at my wife's suggestion, and I've had such fun with it, I have to recommend giving it a shot. Almost immediately, just picturing yourself in a room with those you really admire gives you a big perceptual shift from admiring them to feeling akin to them, almost as peers. In a human sense, it's true — we all are created equal and our notion of someone being great is also our projection onto him or her. They may have had a different opinion of themselves entirely. So, I made a list, and I even drew a little seating arrangement for everyone around my table. And, whenever I like, there they all are, populated by my imagination, doing what they're doing.

I recommend that any serious artist — or anyone serious about seeing an ambitious project all the way through — do this exercise. It helps to have support, and this practice is something we can give ourselves, tapping into parts of our psychology that we project onto other personae. Inviting them to our dinner party helps to connect and ground all parts of us. Napoleon Hill did this exercise for long enough that, over time, he actually received a great deal of input and valuable advice from his group. This could be your result, too, and there's probably no harm in trying. Just assembling them in a room is a fun and inspiring exercise.

1. Brainstorm a list of your favorite things, books, music, paintings, events, writers, and experiences.

2. From that list, invite a handful of people associated with those favorite things. Select only those you really admire to an imaginary dinner party.

3. Whenever you like, you can simply enter that room and find them all there.

4. How does it feel to have them over? How does it feel to share your ideas with them about your book?

# FOLLOWING THE OLD MASTERS

think of old masters as the poet-monks of antiquity who lived alone in small huts in the mountains. Following the tradition of the old masters entails claiming responsibility for my attention span and reaction to life circumstances. It also means not expecting a reward for my efforts, but rather seeing the actions themselves as sufficient for self-realization and liberation. The life lived fully is the responsible one, in which love and creativity are the motivating forces, and the needs of the spirit are fulfilled through action and expression. The heart beats for a reason that I interpret through my thoughts and actions. Its rhythm, when I am attentive to it, inspires me. I am inspired as well by the fact that it goes on beating no matter what I do. Understanding this universality is to touch the sublime — that, expressed simply, it is right to do good even though we don't have to.

The further back I go, the more I tend to know the old masters only through the writing they have left. These were writers and "livers" of poetry because it extended from an overall quest for realization and the experience of tranquility.

# DRIVING TO WORK

Someday I will be clear. I will reach the point where I am self-actualized. I experience satori and the bliss of union. I recognize the wonder and beauty within and around me. As a vessel, I am full and empty. As a stream, I am freely flowing into the ocean. As an individual, I have become wise.

Then what happens? The universe and I are one. And there is work for me to do. There is a new perspective about it; the work is drawn to me. The path opens before me no sooner than I need to take the next step.

There are departures and returns, and each return finds the moment ample, wonderful. The work that the practice continues to take is self-work. I carry forth residues into my practice and rediscover clarity.

Compassion drives me to work, and I am at work in the world, expressing realization within the world's realization.

# IMAGE-RESONANCE STORYTELLING

Sung, spoken, or on the page, poetry is a versatile artifice with intersections into story and crossovers with visual art that can be traced back to hieroglyphs and spells.

Free-form writing is a term for an intent, which may be thought of as artistic because it is creative and places me in a position to experience reality directly, not through the persona of society, prescribed forms of rituals, or other paths of coping with individuation. Writing expresses a moment of clarity that's not encapsulated within this clarity. It speaks through the sensory faculties within the moment in a way that is enlivening, and sheds light.

Good writing can happen through hard work and can occur spontaneously. Writing may be perceived as good for the writer, the reader, or both — one may experience union and self-realization, certainly, by surprise, a surprise that carries recognition with it.

The surprise of recognition is built into the tool of language, just as our bodies have the potential to experience oneness of being through seated contemplation and asana practice, through conversation and action in the world, through the experience of music and of human-to-human, human-to-nature energy.

Running, I am only focused on running, yet I do more than run. I retain thoughts and sensory associations. Breathing the free air in a forest valley, the forest breathes into me more than I breathe it in — the external richness exceeds my intent. Experience changes my alignment and therefore my access to vocabulary. All of it matters, though I only consciously access part of it. That conscious part is the seat where I practice.

We're accustomed to a kind of storytelling that takes us from point A to point Z. It could be that our particular tradition of storytelling accustoms us to this mode; it could also be that when human beings share stories, they do so to get from point A to point Z. However, as is so often the case in life, a need exists to find an empowering and useful sense of balance. I want to be headed somewhere, but I also need to be able to enjoy the journey. When a story imparts the journey for me to enjoy, the experience is fullest — most resonant — when the story pays attention to images that at once ring true and feel fresh (as in, "I never knew anyone could put it that way," or *freshly formed*), yet do not add up to anything and don't supply guidance toward the story's resolution. These are image-resonance stories; they engage a mode of attention that honors the charged and inherently wonderful facets of ordinary experience.

When a story doesn't go someplace, it's not a story, unless it's one of those stories that doesn't go anywhere and seems made to frustrate us into despair and laughter. Stories, like sentences, have structure. Whether a story resonates with me has less to do with its causation and more to do with simple resonance — the energetic relationship of forms against and between other forms.

Each image before us is similar but different. A change of image questions the images that came before. What remains consistent in our minds enacts the ritual of storytelling, whereby, once each frame has passed, it is no longer challenged by our immediate attention and is left to resonate in the pool of recent memory, coloring our interpretation of the next image in the sequence. Just as each moment is fresh, the image carried by the moment is fresh, and because each image interacts (resonates), nothing is ever the same again.

If you were talking to me about dogs, I may be reminded of a story not necessarily about a dog but that has a dog in it. When I tell that story, I take the conversation on a different tangent, but it continues according to resonance.

The purpose of this kind of story is to enliven direct experience. Story ignites upon contact with a significant image. We can't ever know where we'll end up after coming into contact with a significant image. And we don't know what brought us there, because the significant image was not crafted — it emerged.

The only requirement is that each moment be taken as its own full image, and not merely a point along the way that does "work" — foreshadows or establishes character, say. Image-resonance is also useless, as most sensory information in life seems to be useless, having no direct relationship to our goals and ambitions. Yet, when we're attentive to it, life reveals itself as far richer and more wonderful. We see new opportunities or approaches. In storytelling, resonance makes a captivating moment; in life, a mindful one.

Prose poetry and haiku, writing as yoga practice, as an expression of union, point the sentence toward the unknown, yet able to be felt. Whether a phrase strikes or turns in relation to someone has to do with his or her disposition at the moment, as well as with the fact that the phrase is there. The one right way of doing it is the way that honors truth's expression within the exact moment.

Language is connected to the body and is a visceral thing. As the mind and body are one, we relate through the mode of language, trust the moment's expression, adjust to the record kept through writing, and practice further. At some point, story breaks down. This breakdown of story structure is often the best part of the story. Image-resonance storytelling understands that all is one and yet is in love with the details and will continue to search through them.

The love of language, of storytelling, is as old as we are. Images are older still, and they call for us to dissolve into oneness, to become one around a fire, to become one by overcoming the self on a hero's quest. Let us have our expectations upended, laugh without knowing why when things "break into song" in an idea or tonal sense. Let the progression of life from one thing to another bring you along the way to flowering, to love, and perhaps to the attainment of the goal and the arising of a new one. Each pleasant diversion changes who you are. When you return to the path, it is different, because you are.

I celebrate these moments, and I fill my work with them. Continued practice raises my sense of aliveness, and increased aliveness brings the experience of pure awareness. Perceiving with pure awareness brings devotion. Devotion brings enriched attention. Attention brings wisdom. Wisdom brings compassion. Compassion, in turn, raises aliveness. Meditation is not linear.

There is an old story of a renunciate monk who is walking the street after decades of practice. He has re-emerged into the world and is overfull with bliss with all that he sees. A chariot passes by, ornamented, decked in gold, illustrious. The monk beams with joy at the passing chariot of a wealthy man. From the chariot, the wealthy man thinks he sees the joy of ownership reflected in the monk's eyes, and he is baffled. The wealthy man is indignant that this person, laboring for nothing in this world, celebrates with equanimity what he does not own — or does not seem to have purchased.

The wealthy man comes to realize that the monk welcomes all of life's manifestations equally as they pass by him. The wealthy man's position in the world hid equanimity from him. Surrounded by the image of wealth, he was unable to relish in it and beyond it with naked satisfaction.

In free-form practice, we glimpse the understanding that we do not need to feel separate from the wild force of nature — we understand how it breathes into us, interpenetrates our entire physical self. We are nature's children. There is no part of you or any material thing that doesn't exist within nature. Nature has no beginning or end, no separation, no ownership. Wild nature is infinite. You are that.

# ABOUT THE AUTHOR

Stephen Lloyd Webber earned an MFA in poetry from New Mexico State University and founded Writing Immersion Retreats, teaching several yoga and writing intensives each year in Italy, Bali, and the Caribbean. His essays, fiction, poetry, and book reviews have appeared in numerous literary magazines. He has studied yoga under the Pranakriya/Kripalu tradition under Yoganand Michael Carroll. See *summerwritingretreat.com*.

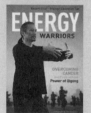

### YEAR ZERO: *Time of the Great Shift*
by Kiara Windrider

"I can barely contain myself as I implode with gratitude for the gift of *Year Zero*! Every word resonates on a cellular level, awakening ancient memories and realigning my consciousness with an unshakable knowing that the best has yet to come. This is more than a book; it is a manual for building the new world!"

— Mikki Willis, founder, ELEVATE

### ILAHINOOR: *Awakening the Divine Human*
by Kiara Windrider

"Ilahinoor is a truly precious and powerful gift for those yearning to receive and integrate Kiara Windrider's guidance on their journey for spiritual awakening and wisdom surrounding the planet's shifting process."

— Alexandra Delis-Abrams, Ph.D., author *Attitudes, Beliefs, and Choices*

### THE MESSAGE: *A Guide to Being Human*
by LD Thompson

"Simple, profound, and moving! The author has been given a gift... a beautiful way to distill the essence of life into an easy-to-read set of truths, with wonderful examples along the way. Listen... for that is how it all starts."

— Lee Carroll, author, the *Kryon* series; co-author, *The Indigo Children*

### SOPHIA—THE FEMININE FACE OF GOD:
*Nine Heart Paths to Healing and Abundance*

by Karen Speerstra

"Karen Speerstra shows us most compellingly that when we open our hearts, we discover the wisdom of the Feminine all around us. A totally refreshing exploration, and beautifully researched read."

— Michael Cecil, author, *Living at the Heart of Creation*

### A FULLER VIEW: *Buckminster Fuller's Vision of Hope and Abundance for All*
by L. Steven Sieden

"This book elucidates Buckminster Fuller's thinking, honors his spirit, and creates an enthusiasm for continuing his work."

— Marianne Williamson, author, *Return To Love* and *Healing the Soul of America*

### GAIA CALLS: *South Sea Voices, Dolphins, Sharks & Rainforests*
by Wade Daok

"Wade has the soul of a dolphin, and has spent a life on and under the oceans on a quest for deep knowledge. This is an important book that will change our views of the ocean and our human purpose."

— Ric O'Barry, author, *Behind the Dolphin Smile* and star of *The Cove*, which won the 2010 Academy Award for Best Documentary

**1.800.833.5738 • 25% discount available online • www.divineartsmedia.com**

# DIVINE
## ARTS

DIVINE ARTS sprang to life fully formed as an intention to bring spiritual practice into daily living. Human beings are far more than the one-dimensional creatures perceived by most of humanity and held static in consensus reality. There is a deep and vast body of knowledge — both ancient and emerging — that informs and gives us the understanding, through direct experience, that we are magnificent creatures occupying many dimensions with untold powers and connectedness to all that is. Divine Arts books and films explore these realms, powers and teachings through inspiring, informative and empowering works by pioneers, artists and great teachers from all the wisdom traditions.

We invite your participation and look forward to learning how we may better serve you.

Onward and upward,

Michael Wiese
Publisher/Filmmaker

DivineArtsMedia.com